Longman Science 11–13 Series
General Editor: John L. Lewis

Also in this series: **Biology 11–13**
Physics 11–13

CHEMISTRY 11-13

F. O. Harriss M.A.
Head of Chemistry Department, Malvern College

H. J. C. Ferguson M.A., Ph.D.
Malvern College
Formerly Head of Chemistry Department

Longman

Preface

This book is for boys and girls in their first two years of a modern chemistry course. It concentrates on explaining the ideas rather than presenting a vast amount of factual information. Practical instructions are not included as we feel that individual teachers would prefer to select their own experiments and issue their own instructions. However, constant reference is made to experiments and experimental results, and the book will be most useful to pupils in helping them to summarize and tie together their experimental deductions.

We feel that this presentation of chemistry as a coherent whole, rather than as a series of unanswered questions, will help pupils to work on their own and lead them to a greater understanding. To test this understanding a large number of questions are included.

The text should be particularly useful for those approaching chemistry as an academic study and those needing to revise for an examination.

Our thanks are due to T. C. Swinfen (Uppingham School), H. J. Dixon (Mostyn House, Wirral), H. J. Jannion (Wells House, Malvern) and especially to J. A. H. Porch (Maidwell Hall, Northampton) for reading the manuscript and making many helpful suggestions. We are also grateful to Kirsten Campbell-Ferguson for typing the manuscript.

We would be pleased to know of any errors which the book contains, and we would be grateful for suggestions as to how it could be improved.

Malvern 1978   F. O. Harriss
H. J. Campbell-Ferguson

Contents

Everything

Chapter 1 # The separation and purification of solids

1.1 Introduction

Life today depends on industry and modern industry requires raw materials. These are rarely found in pure form. Substances which occur naturally are usually **mixtures** of chemicals: the air is a mixture, the sea is a mixture, rocks are often mixtures. Even a human being is a very complicated mixture of chemical substances! It is the task of the chemist to purify substances for use in industry and elsewhere.

Many chemicals do not occur naturally and have to be made from other substances which we do possess. This, too, is the chemist's job. When he carries out an experiment he will need pure substances. The purification of substances is thus an important part of chemistry. This Chapter describes some of the simple methods which can be used to purify chemicals.

1.2 Water, ice and steam

Before we can talk about purification we must consider the three 'states' in which substances are found. We will take water as an example.

If we cool water it **freezes** when a temperature of zero degrees centigrade (0°C) is reached. It becomes 'solid water' which we call **ice**. When water is heated it boils when the temperature reaches 100°C and turns into **steam**. This process is known as **evaporation**. So we know that water exists in three states: solid, liquid and gas. This is summarized in Fig 1.1. You will see that the opposite of freezing is **melting**. The opposite of evaporation is

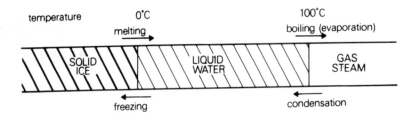

Fig 1.1 Ice, water and steam

condensation (that is, cooling a gas until it becomes a liquid).

Other substances also exist in the three 'states': solid, liquid and gas. However, the temperatures at which they melt and boil are different from those of water (see Section 3.2).

1.3 The purification of rock salt

One of the commonest chemicals is salt (in chemical language, sodium chloride). This occurs in vast quantities in sea water. It has also been deposited on land as a result of the evaporation of the water from seas which existed millions of years ago. Rock salt is the name given to dirty brown salt crystals which are obviously impure. They can be purified in a simple experiment.

Take a small amount of rock salt and grind up the crystals using a pestle and mortar (Fig 1.2a). Put the small crystals in warm water in a beaker (Fig 1.2b) or large test-tube (Fig 1.2c), and stir them until they dissolve. (The process takes longer if the crystals are large or the water is cold.) The solid brown dirt does not dissolve.

Then pour the mixture through a piece of filter paper placed in a filter funnel (Fig 1.2d). The brown dirt will remain on the paper, while the salt water will pass through it into a suitable vessel such as an evaporating basin (Fig 1.2e). This process is called **filtration**.

Take the solution which has passed through the filter paper into the evaporating basin and heat it until crystals begin to form at the edges. Continue the evaporation slowly

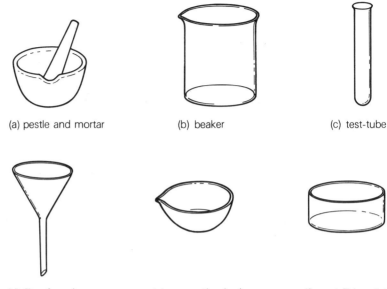

(a) pestle and mortar   (b) beaker   (c) test-tube

Fig 1.2 Some simple apparatus   (d) filter funnel   (e) evaporating basin   (f) crystallizing dish

and cubic crystals of salt will form. Before the evaporation is complete, filter the contents of the basin. Wash the salt crystals with a little cold water and dry them with coarse filter paper or blotting paper. They are now pure salt.

Let us look at these steps in more detail. They are illustrated in Fig 1.3.

Dissolving

Fig 1.3 The purification of rock salt

When salt dissolves in water, the solution formed appears to

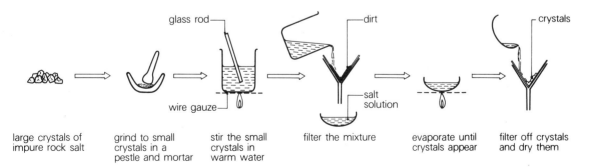

large crystals of impure rock salt → grind to small crystals in a pestle and mortar → stir the small crystals in warm water → filter the mixture → evaporate until crystals appear → filter off crystals and dry them

glass rod — wire gauze —   dirt — salt solution   crystals

be very similar to water itself and it seems as if the salt has disappeared. However, we know that this is *not* so for several reasons:

1. The solution tastes salty.
2. We can get the salt back again by evaporation.
3. If we try to freeze the solution we find that it does not freeze at 0°C, but several degrees lower. The addition of salt to water has lowered the freezing point. This is why salt is sprinkled on icy roads in winter.
4. The solution boils at a higher temperature than 100°C (the boiling point of pure water).

The salt has **dissolved** in the water to form a **solution**. The solution is a mixture of the solid and water; the salt is known as the **solute** and the water as the **solvent**. The salt is **soluble** in the water whereas the brown dirt is insoluble. The large salt crystals have been split up into very small, invisible particles which have spread out through the water to form the solution.

If an **insoluble** substance is shaken with water a **suspension** results. You must be careful to distinguish between solutions, which are clear (transparent), and suspensions, which are cloudy until the visible particles have had time to settle. Many medicines and lotions are suspensions. 'Calamine lotion' is an example. After a while the white solid sinks to the bottom, leaving a clear solution above it. We are instructed to 'shake the bottle' to make a suspension before we use the lotion.

Filtration

In solutions the water particles and the dissolved particles are very small and pass through a filter paper. However, the particles of solid in a suspension are larger and are trapped on the filter paper. This solid is called the **residue** while the clear liquid which comes through the filter is called the **filtrate**. Thus, in the purification of rock salt, the residue is the brown dirt and the filtrate is the salt solution.

As an alternative to filtration, a machine called a centrifuge can be used. The test-tube is spun very fast and the solid goes to the bottom of the tube. The liquid can then be poured off.

Evaporation and crystallization

To separate solid salt from its solution, the solution can be heated. The water turns into steam, but the salt is unaffected. The water evaporates (turns from liquid into gas) and the solution becomes more **concentrated**.

There is a limit to the amount of salt which can be dissolved in a given quantity of water. A solution in which no more salt will dissolve is said to be **saturated** with salt. When enough water has evaporated from a salt solution, a saturated solution forms. As more water evaporates the salt starts to **crystallize** since there is no longer enough water to dissolve all the salt. Crystallization is often carried out in a crystallizing dish (Fig 1.2f).

Once the crystals have been formed they are separated from the remaining solution by filtration to stop any soluble impurities crystallizing. The crystals are then washed with water (to wash off any dissolved impurities) and dried.

1.4 The purification of other solids

Many solids are soluble in water and can be purified by using the method described in Section 1.2. For example, alum crystals can be purified in the same way as salt. The crystals can be obtained by allowing a hot saturated solution to cool slowly. Alum is much more soluble in hot water than in cold water; so a lot of crystals form as the solution cools.

However, some solids are insoluble in water. For example, mothballs are made of naphthalene which is insoluble in water. So instead of water we use a different solvent in which naphthalene does dissolve: there are several possible ones, but acetone is usually chosen.

Other non-aqueous solvents (solvents which contain no water) are carbon tetrachloride (tetrachloromethane), ethanol, chloroform (trichloromethane) and ether. Many of these are flammable (catch fire easily) or poisonous, so care must be taken when using them. To purify a solid, a solvent must be found which dissolves the pure substance but does not dissolve the impurities. The most suitable solvent can be

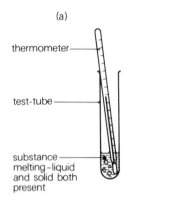

(a)

thermometer

test-tube

substance melting - liquid and solid both present

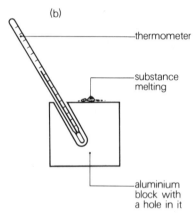

(b)

thermometer

substance melting

aluminium block with a hole in it

Fig 1.4 Finding melting points
– 2 methods

decided by 'trial and error' experiments. The solid is dissolved in the solvent, the mixture is filtered and the solvent is evaporated: just as we did when purifying salt, using water as the solvent.

When a solid has been purified, its purity can be proved by finding its **melting point**. Two simple apparatuses for doing this are shown in Fig 1.4. In Fig 1.4a the substance is placed in a test-tube which is gently heated until the solid begins to melt. In Fig 1.4b the solid is ground up and a few very small crystals are placed on the aluminium block which is heated gently so that the temperature rises slowly. If all the crystals suddenly melt at a certain temperature which is known to be the melting point of the substance (for example 0°C for water, 80°C for naphthalene), then the substance is pure. But if melting occurs over a range of temperatures *below* the known melting point, the substance is impure and the purification process must be repeated.

1.5 Chromatography

Some solids can be separated and purified by a method known as **chromatography**. Grass, for example, contains a number of dyes which are insoluble in water but which dissolve in other solvents such as acetone. A concentrated solution of the colouring matter in grass is made and a drop of this is placed on a piece of filter paper (Fig 1.5). The pure solvent is then allowed to move up or along the paper and the different dyes are separated. The paper can either be supported horizontally and the drop placed in the middle (Fig 1.5a), or horizontally with a 'tongue' up which the solvent can travel (Fig 1.5b) or vertically with the spot about 2 cm from the bottom (Fig 1.5c). In the case of grass, the yellow xanthophyll travels furthest, followed by the green chlorophyll and finally the orange carotene. The separation can be improved if solvents other than acetone are used.

Separation occurs for two reasons. If several dyes are put into a particular solvent, some of them will dissolve more than others; the better they dissolve, the further they travel on the paper. Also the paper absorbs different dyes to different extents. So there is a 'tug of war' between the paper

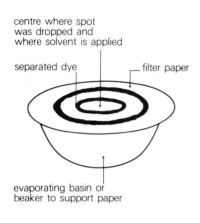

centre where spot
was dropped and
where solvent is applied

separated dye — filter paper

evaporating basin or
beaker to support paper

(a) Horizontal

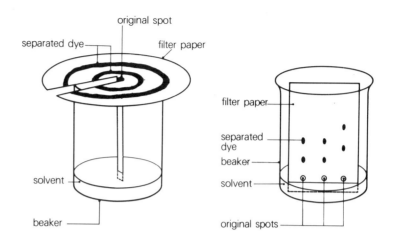

original spot

separated dye — filter paper

solvent

beaker

(b) Horizontal with tongue

filter paper —

separated
dye —

beaker —

solvent —

original spots —

(c) Vertical

Fig 1.5 Chromatography

(trying to hold the dye at the starting point) and the solvent (trying to pull the dye along with it). This 'tug of war' decides how far the dye will move relative to the distance travelled by the solvent.

Chromatography is also suitable for coloured inks, when water can sometimes be used as a solvent. Inks in felt-tip pens often contain several dyes.

After chromatography has taken place the piece of paper is known as a **chromatogram**. Chromatograms can be used to discover which dyes a particular mixture contains. Fig 1.6 gives an example of a chromatogram which could be used to investigate three orange dyes. Spots of three orange dyes, C, D and E, are placed on the start line and also spots of a red dye, A, and a yellow dye, B, which might be present in the orange dyes. The chromatogram is then placed in a large beaker with a layer of solvent at the bottom (as in Fig 1.3c). The solvent rises up the paper and the dyes follow to varying extents, each dye staying as a spot. When the solvent has reached the top of the paper, the spots of dyes have reached the positions shown in Fig 1.6.

The results show that the orange dye, D, is a mixture of two dyes since it separates into two spots. The red dye is A, as the spots of red dye and A have risen to the same height;

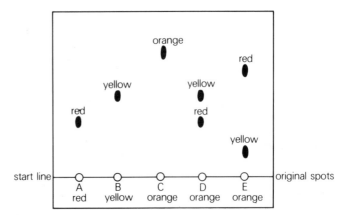

Fig 1.6 A chromatogram

the yellow dye is B for similar reasons. Dye C gives only one spot and is probably a pure orange dye rather than a mixture of yellow and red. E is a mixture, but the red dye is not the same as A because the spot does not rise to the same height; nor is the yellow dye B.

Chromatography is not suitable for separating large quantities of dyes and so other methods must be used instead. One method is fractional distillation which is described in the next Chapter.

Summary

1. Substances exist in three states: solid, liquid and gas.
2. Many impure solids can be purified by dissolving them in water and filtering to remove insoluble impurities. The solution is then evaporated or allowed to crystallize. Sometimes other solvents are used instead of water.
3. A pure substance melts at one temperature. An impure substance melts over a range of temperatures.
4. Chromatography can be used to separate mixtures of coloured substances.

Questions

1.† Salt and iron filings can be separated by adding them to warm water. What must then be done to obtain pure salt in this experiment? Why would this method *not* be suitable for a mixture of salt and sugar?

2. When salt is purified, explain why:
a. The impure salt is crushed.
b. The impure solution is filtered.
c. The solution is heated after it has been filtered.

3.†
a. You wish to make a concentrated solution of lump rock salt in water as quickly as possible. State three things you would do to hasten the process.
b. Explain simply why any one of them is effective.

4.† When a boy was asked to find out whether chalk was soluble in water, he added water to some chalk, filtered the mixture and transferred one drop of the clear liquid to a microscope slide. After evaporation of water a trace of white solid remained on the slide.
a. What can he deduce from this experiment?
b. What was the reason for filtering the mixture?

5.†
a. When fructose, a sweet compound derived from certain fruits, is added to water at room temperature, it seems to disappear. A possible explanation for this is: the fructose .... in the water. Choose the word which would fill the gap.
   Condenses, crystallizes, dissolves, evaporates, melts.
b. In an attempt to find out whether stirring increased the rate of disappearance of the fructose in the water, equal masses of fructose were put in separate containers with equal volumes of water and stirred at different rates. The times for the complete disappearance of the fructose were as given below:
   Rate of stirring (revs per minute)   0   5   10
   Time of disappearance (minutes)   10   6   2
   Did increasing the rate of stirring increase, decrease or have no effect on the rate of disappearance of the fructose?
c. Why was it considered necessary to keep the masses of fructose and the volumes of water the same in all three experiments?
d. Write a brief set of instructions for a method of finding out whether or not the rate of disappearance depends on the temperature of the mixture.

6. Benzoic acid is a white solid which is insoluble in cold water, but soluble in hot water.

Charcoal is insoluble in cold and hot water.

a. Explain the steps by which you would obtain pure benzoic acid from a mixture of benzoic acid and charcoal.

b. How would you show that the benzoic acid crystals were pure?

c. Salt is soluble in cold water. How would you obtain pure benzoic acid from a mixture of benzoic acid, charcoal and salt?

7. Sand is insoluble in water and insoluble in carbon tetrachloride. Common salt is soluble in water, but insoluble in carbon tetrachloride. Wax is insoluble in water, but soluble in carbon tetrachloride.

You are given a mixture of sand, common salt and wax. How would you obtain a pure sample of each of them?

8. Naphthalene melts at 80°C and becomes liquid naphthalene. Liquid naphthalene and a solution of naphthalene are both colourless liquids.

a. What is the difference between liquid naphthalene and a solution of naphthalene?

b. How would you obtain naphthalene crystals from a solution of naphthalene?

c. How would you obtain solid naphthalene from liquid naphthalene?

9. Tincture of iodine is a disinfectant, and is made by dissolving crystals of iodine in dilute alcohol. Name:
a. The solvent. b. The solute. c. The solution.

10.†

	Solvent A	Solvent B
Substance X	soluble	insoluble
Substance Y	insoluble	soluble

Suggest names for the solvents A and B and the substances X and Y.

11.† A blackcurrant-flavoured ice-lolly is coloured purple. Write the instructions for an experiment to find out whether it contained a purple food colouring or a mixture of a red and a blue one.

12.†

a. A green solution is said to contain a number of compounds which are coloured differently. How would you test this statement?

b. You are given a sample of naphthalene, a white solid that melts easily. What experiment would you carry out in order to test whether it is pure?

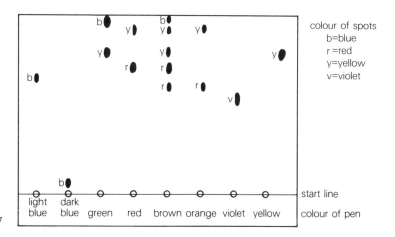

Fig 1.7

13. The chromatogram in Fig 1.7 was obtained using a set of felt-tip pens and water as the solvent.

a. Which pens contained only one dye?

b. Green can be obtained by mixing blue and yellow. Has the manufacturer done this? Has he used the light blue, the dark blue or a different blue altogether? Give your reasons.

c. Brown can be obtained by mixing red and green. What did the manufacturer do?

d. Is the yellow used in the orange pen the same that is used in the green pen? How many different yellows have been used in the eight pens?

e. Which of the dyes is likely to be the least soluble in water?

f. This experiment was carried out at home in the holidays. Explain how you would obtain such a chromatogram using only materials that can be found in the home.

11

Background reading

Crystals

Many solids are much more soluble in hot solvents than in cold solvents. An example is a white solid called alum. When a hot solution of alum in water cools, crystals start to form. This is because the solid is less soluble in cold water than it is in hot water, so some of it comes out of solution. Common salt is slightly exceptional in that its solubility in water does not alter much with temperature and so it is necessary to get rid of some of the water (by evaporation) to allow salt crystals to form.

The size of crystals can be adjusted by cooling the solution at different rates. Slow cooling produces one or two large crystals, while fast cooling gives many very small crystals. This can be seen in experiments using copper sulphate or potassium nitrate. Larger crystals of salt can be grown by allowing the water to evaporate slowly at room temperature rather than by boiling off the water, but this takes a long time.

A really large crystal of copper sulphate can be grown by taking a small crystal of copper sulphate and suspending it in a saturated solution of copper sulphate (a solution which contains as much copper sulphate as possible) and allowing the water to evaporate slowly. This process can be repeated as the crystal becomes bigger.

Crystals have many different shapes, and substances therefore tend to crystallize separately. An exception to this is the alums which all crystallize as octahedra (double square pyramids). If a purple chrome alum crystal is suspended in a colourless saturated solution of potash alum, it will gain a colourless layer.

Crystals also form when substances freeze; such crystals tend to form quickly and can be studied under a low power microscope. Salol (phenyl salicylate) crystallizes well and you may also have seen the beautiful crystalline forms of water in snow flakes.

Question

Given a supply of very small crystals of iron alum (which is fairly soluble in cold water and very soluble in hot water), how would you attempt to grow a large crystal of iron alum?

For further reading on crystals, see *Physics 11–13*, Chapter 2.

Dry-cleaning
The solvent which is used for most cleaning purposes is water. Not only has this the advantage of being cheap but it can also dissolve more substances than any other solvent. It is used to wash clothes, dishes and people. The washing process can usually be made more efficient if a small amount of a soap or a detergent is added. This aids the removal of grease which is insoluble in pure water.

Some objects would be damaged by the use of water to clean them, for example parts of engines and certain articles of clothing, such as jackets. In these cases dry-cleaning is used which involves the use of a solvent other than water. For clothing trichloroethane ('tri-chloro-ethane') is used. This has the advantage that it is non-flammable (does not catch fire) and its vapour is not poisonous in small quantities. It dissolves the grease which has absorbed dirt and thus the dirt is freed from the fabric. After use the remaining solvent quickly evaporates leaving the clothing clean.

Questions
1. Name a substance which might be present in dirty clothes and which is soluble in water.
2. Why might:
a. parts of engines,
b. jackets
   be damaged by washing with water?
3. Why is it important that a dry-cleaning solvent is non-flammable and not poisonous?
4. Name another solvent which could be used for dry-cleaning. Is it as suitable as trichloroethane?

Chapter 2 # Separation and purification of liquids

2.1 Immiscible liquids

Just as some solids are insoluble in some solvents, so some liquids mix together and some do not. Those that do not mix are said to be **immiscible**. Water is immiscible with many liquids such as paraffin and carbon tetrachloride (tetrachloromethane).

The separation of immiscible liquids is very simple. The mixture is placed in a separating funnel (Fig 2.1) where the less dense one will form the upper layer. The two liquids can be run out of the funnel one after the other.

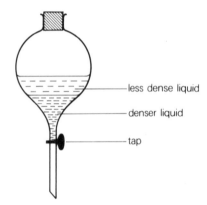

less dense liquid

denser liquid

tap

Fig 2.1 A separating funnel

2.2 Distillation

If the liquids mix (for example water and ethanol) or if we have a solution of a solid in a liquid, the problem is more difficult and we have to use distillation. Consider first how to obtain a pure liquid from a solution of a solid in the liquid. If the solution is evaporated, only the liquid boils off and the solid remains behind (Section 1.3). If the vapour* is condensed (turned back to a liquid) we shall have achieved our aim. The process of evaporation followed by condensation is called **distillation**. A very simple apparatus for distillation is shown in Fig 2.2. **Anti-bumping granules** (small pieces of unreactive material) are added to prevent violent boiling which is known as **bumping**. This apparatus is inefficient because the tube soon warms up and so the vapour no longer condenses. An improvement is to

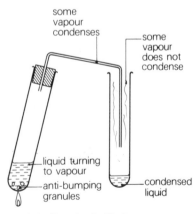

some vapour condenses

some vapour does not condense

liquid turning to vapour

anti-bumping granules

condensed liquid

Fig 2.2 Simple distillation

* The word vapour is often used to refer to a gas which can easily be condensed back to a liquid.

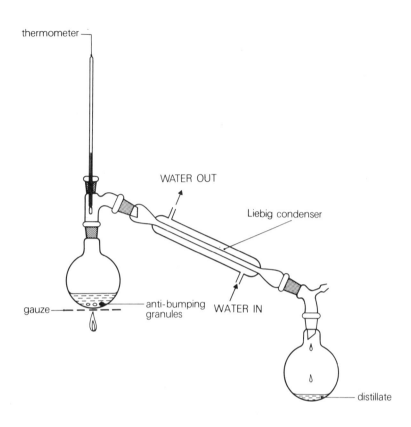

Fig 2.3 Distillation using a Liebig condenser

thermometer

WATER OUT

Liebig condenser

gauze

anti-bumping granules

WATER IN

distillate

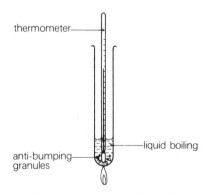

thermometer

anti-bumping granules

liquid boiling

Fig 2.4 Measuring a boiling point

surround this tube with a beaker of cold water, but this also heats up and has to be replaced. A more efficient piece of apparatus is the Liebig condenser which uses a continual stream of cold water flowing in an outer jacket (Fig 2.3). The water should enter this at the bottom so that the jacket is always full. Then a slow rate of flow can be used.

If copper sulphate solution or ink are distilled, the liquid which condenses (the distillate) is colourless and we presume it is pure water. This can be tested by measuring its boiling point using the apparatus shown in Fig 2.4. The temperature of the water rises as it is heated and then remains steady – this is the boiling point. Water boils around 100°C (the exact temperature depends on the atmospheric pressure). If the boiling temperature increases during the distillation then the distillate is a mixture of liquids rather

15

than one pure liquid. Great care must be taken when distilling liquids other than water since they are often flammable (catch fire easily) or poisonous.

2.3 Fractional distillation

What do you think would happen if a mixture of ethanol (b.p. 79°C) and water (b.p. 100°C) (two miscible liquids) were distilled in the apparatus of Fig 2.3? Quite a reasonable

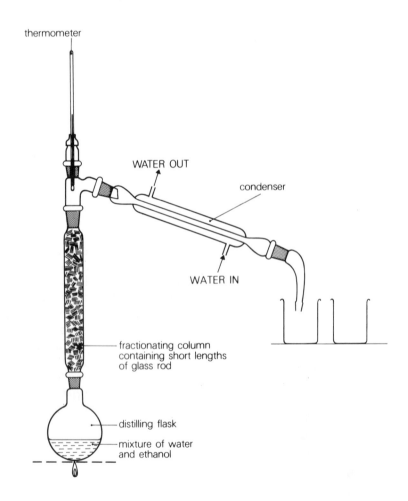

thermometer

WATER OUT

condenser

WATER IN

fractionating column containing short lengths of glass rod

distilling flask

mixture of water and ethanol

Fig 2.5 Fractional distillation of a mixture of water and ethanol

answer might be that the ethanol, having a lower boiling point, would boil off first, leaving the water. However this does not happen; the distillate consists of a mixture of ethanol and water, but it has a slightly higher proportion of ethanol than the original mixture. If this distillate were distilled, the new distillate would be richer in ethanol. This process could be repeated, but it is a very laborious way of separating the mixture. However in the apparatus shown in Fig 2.5 this process of continual distillation does occur. The mixture of ethanol and water vapours rises to a certain point and condenses. The liquid drops down a little. There the temperature is hotter, so it boils again. The vapour rises, but it condenses not far above the place where it condensed before. Thus in the column a very large number of 'evaporation then condensation' steps occur. Each time the vapour gets a little richer in ethanol. So, if the column is big enough, almost pure ethanol vapour comes out at the top. (Ethanol and water cannot be separated completely by distillation.) The column is called a **fractionating column** because it divides mixtures of liquids into parts or fractions according to their boiling point. This process is called **fractional distillation**.

The initial step in the refining of petroleum (crude oil) is fractional distillation. Because crude oil contains hundreds of compounds, pure liquids are not produced; instead 'fractions' are obtained. In each fraction are all the compounds which boil within a certain temperature range. In the laboratory experiment (Fig 2.6) the test-tube itself acts as the fractionating column.

Gentle heating of the crude oil gives the first fraction, boiling between room temperature and about 70°C. It is very **volatile** (turns easily to a gas), very flammable and can be poured easily. As heating continues other fractions may be collected, until the last (boiling above about 180°C) is involatile, cannot be burnt and is very **viscous** (treacly). In addition it is usually darker in colour. The fractions are not pure substances: this can be seen from the fact that the temperature rises as a particular sample is being collected. The fractions are still mixtures of compounds, but each fraction contain a group of substances with similar boiling points. Thus the fractions behave differently from one another.

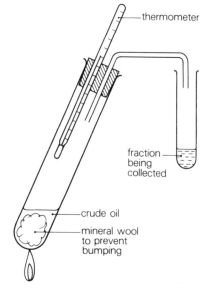

thermometer

fraction being collected

crude oil

mineral wool to prevent bumping

Fig 2.6 Simple laboratory distillation of crude oil

2.4 Industrial distillation of oil

Petroleum is separated into its different fractions using a fractionating tower (Fig 2.7). The most volatile components go to the top of the tower. At each level it becomes cooler and some of the compounds in oil condense. The remainder

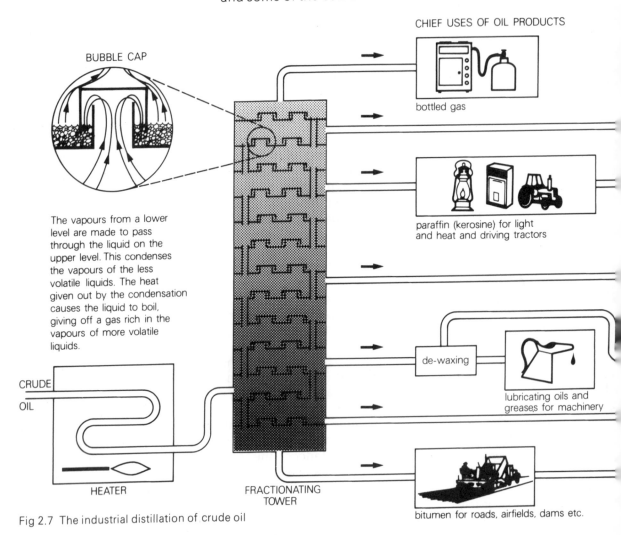

CHIEF USES OF OIL PRODUCTS

BUBBLE CAP

The vapours from a lower level are made to pass through the liquid on the upper level. This condenses the vapours of the less volatile liquids. The heat given out by the condensation causes the liquid to boil, giving off a gas rich in the vapours of more volatile liquids.

CRUDE OIL

HEATER

FRACTIONATING TOWER

bottled gas

paraffin (kerosine) for light and heat and driving tractors

de-waxing

lubricating oils and greases for machinery

bitumen for roads, airfields, dams etc.

Fig 2.7 The industrial distillation of crude oil

continue to rise, as gases, to higher levels. The liquid at each level can fall to a lower level; the temperature is higher there and so the most volatile compounds will again turn into gases.

Distillation is only the first process in the refining of petroleum and further processes are used to obtain the products we need. Fuel for motor cars comes from the gasoline fraction and jet aeroplane fuel comes from the

EXAMPLES OF OTHER USES

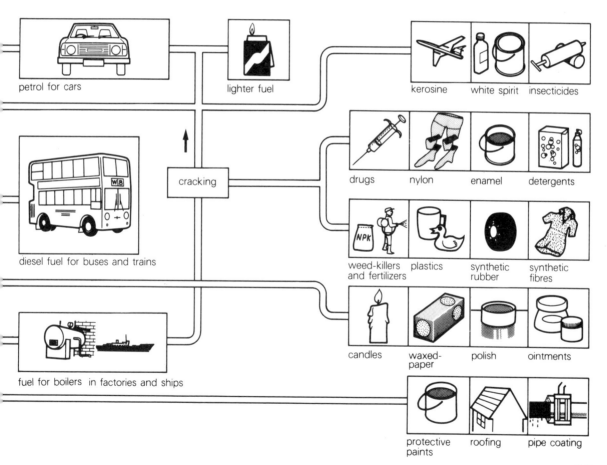

petrol for cars

lighter fuel

kerosine   white spirit   insecticides

cracking

drugs   nylon   enamel   detergents

diesel fuel for buses and trains

weed-killers and fertilizers   plastics   synthetic rubber   synthetic fibres

candles   waxed-paper   polish   ointments

fuel for boilers in factories and ships

protective paints   roofing   pipe coating

kerosene fraction. The heavy oils are used to make fuel oil for ships and bitumen for roads, though a further process, known as cracking, can break down these heavy oils to produce gasoline and the raw materials for plastics.

2.5 Distillation of air

The air is a mixture of gases and these can be separated by cooling air until it condenses and then fractionally distilling the resulting liquid air. Carbon dioxide and water vapour are removed first.

The method of condensation relies on the fact that gases cool when allowed to expand suddenly. You may have noticed this when making soda water with carbon dioxide. The opposite effect is that air tends to warm up when compressed and you may have felt this happening when pumping up your bicycle tyres.

Air is compressed, cooled and then allowed to expand suddenly so that it gets very cold and becomes liquid. If the liquid is allowed to warm up in a fractionating column the various gases can be separated, though there are difficulties because the boiling points of the substances are so close to each other. The composition of the air is given in Chapter 5.

Summary
1. Immiscible liquids can be separated using a separating funnel.
2. The solvent can be separated from a solution by distillation, which involves evaporation and condensation.
3. Mixtures of liquids can be separated by fractional distillation using a fractionating column.
4. Fractional distillation is used in industry to separate crude oil and liquid air into their components.

Questions
1.† Give the names of the processes which you would use to separate the following substances from the following mixtures:

a. Sand from a suspension of sand in salt solution.
b. Water from copper sulphate solution.
c. A red dye from a mixture of red, blue and yellow dyes.

2.†
a. Give an example of a solvent which contains no water.
b. Give an example of a solute that dissolves in this solvent.
c. What is the name given to the process by which you could recover a solvent from a solution?

3.† You and a friend decide to produce some drinking water from a bucket of dirty sea water.
a. Your friend says he can easily get the bits of seaweed and dirt out. What does he do?
b. You say you can remove the salt. What do you do with the clean sea water to make it tasteless? (Draw a diagram of the apparatus you would use.)
c. Your friend claims that sea-salt is better for you than ordinary salt. How would you obtain a sample of dry sea-salt crystals from your sea water?

4. Royal blue ink can be distilled to produce a colourless liquid which boils at 100°C.
a. Draw a diagram of simple apparatus that could be used in this experiment.
b. A Liebig condenser can be used to make the distillation more efficient. Draw a diagram of such a condenser and explain how it works.
c. What is the distillate (the colourless liquid that boils at 100°C)?
d. What has happened to the dyes in the ink?
e. What experiment would you do to find out how many dyes there are in the ink?

5. How would you obtain:
a. Sand from gritty sea water?
b. Salt from sea water?
c. Pure water from sea water?
d. Water from a mixture of petrol and water? (Petrol does not dissolve in water.)
e. Petrol from a mixture of petrol and water?
f. The colours in a copper beech leaf?

6. Universal indicator consists of a number of dyes dissolved in ethanol.
a. How would you try to separate the dyes?
b. How would you obtain ethanol from universal indicator?
c. How would you show that the liquid you obtained was ethanol?

7.[†] In an essay on petroleum a boy wrote: 'Crude oil can be distilled into many different fractions, with the lighter, more volatile fractions coming off first.'
Explain briefly the meaning of the following words:
a. Crude.
b. Distilled.
c. Volatile.

8. This is an extract from an article entitled 'The Holy Water of Ireland' from *The Daily Telegraph Colour Supplement, 14.8.1970*. Read it carefully and answer the questions below.

Inside the barn the first of two stills was being set up on bits of breeze block, leaving a space for the gas ring underneath. First, next to the door was the steel drum into which the wash was poured, a bucket at a time, from the barrels outside. In the top of the oil drum a neat circular hole held the still-head, a bottomless wooden bucket with its top covered over. From a hole in the side of the still-head the conical arm sloped gradually down to the cooling barrel where it joined the head of the five-bend 'worm'. The copper worm disappeared beneath the surface of the cool brown spring water in the wooden barrel to emerge from a small hole at the bottom ...

The stills were now ready and the gas cylinders were brought in and connected, a bright blue flame roaring up beneath the two oil drums. There was little to do now but watch and wait till the first run, the 'singlings' started to come over. Seamus adjusted the heat carefully so that it would bring off the alcohol and leave the water behind ... We sat and watched until a brown liquid started to trickle from the end of the first worm. Seamus bent and tasted it with his finger. The heat was too great and it was not coming off strong enough. He lowered the gas and threw a couple of buckets of water over the side of the drum to cool it a little . . .

He tasted it again. 'That's it, the singlings', he said, and put a bucket beneath to catch the impure whiskey.

a. This process could obviously be carried out in laboratory apparatus. Give the names of the pieces of equipment which would correspond to:
  i The steel drum (line 3).
  ii The worm and cooling barrel (lines 9 and 10).
b. Draw a diagram of the still described above as you imagine it might look.
c. How would you explain to Seamus, in simple terms:
  i Why lowering the temperature produced more alcohol in the singlings.
  ii Why he might have to change the water in the cooling barrel occasionally.
d. What do you think the 'wash' might have been made from?
e. Before the very strong 'worm beer' is produced, which is diluted to make the final whiskey, another distillation is carried out. Why do you think this is?

9.
a. Draw a diagram of an apparatus suitable for distilling a small quantity of crude oil in the laboratory, so as to separate it into about four fractions. Label your diagram.
b. There would be a risk of fire in distilling a fairly large bulk of crude oil in the laboratory. Mention one way in which this risk could be minimized.
c. How does the first fraction differ from the last fraction in:
  i Colour?
  ii Flammability?
  iii Viscosity?
d. Why would the last fraction be unsuitable as fuel for a motor car? What properties does motor car fuel have?
e. Give one reason for believing that each of the four fractions is a mixture rather than a pure substance.

10.

a. Where in an oil refinery would you find a 'bubble-cap'? How does a bubble-cap work?

b. A volatile substance in crude oil enters a fractionating tower. Why does it rise to the top?

c. An involatile substance in crude oil enters the tower. Why does it go to the bottom?

11. Use your library and reference books to help you to answer the following questions.

a. How do oil men set about looking for oil?

b. How do they test their theory that an oilfield exists in a certain place?

c. How do they get the oil to the surface?

d. How do they take the oil from the well to the refinery or nearest port?

Background reading

Using distillation to make alcoholic drinks (spirits)

Starch or sugar can be turned into ethanol (alcohol) by a process called **fermentation**. This is carried out by the micro-organism yeast. When barley is fermented beer is formed, and fermented grapes give wine. However an ethanol concentration of over 15% cannot be obtained by fermentation, as this alcohol level 'kills' the yeast. In order to make drinks with a higher alcohol content, the liquids made by fermentation are **distilled**. The drinks which result from distillation are called spirits.

The distillation of a mixture of ethanol and water is discussed in Section 2.3. If the correct conditions are used an ethanol–water mixture containing a high proportion of ethanol can be produced. (This is illegal without an excise licence.) The solution also contains the other volatile materials present in the original liquids which give the characteristic taste. In the case of whisky, the drink is then diluted with water to about 40% alcohol, and colouring matter is added. Different countries have produced different spirits, and all have been responsible for much alcoholism though they give pleasure to those who sample them in moderation.

Country	Drink	Made from
Scotland	whisky	barley
France	brandy	wine (grapes)
Holland	gin	corn (flavoured with juniper)
West Indies	rum	molasses (sugar cane)
Scandinavia	snaps	potatoes
Russia	vodka	corn or potatoes

Liqueurs are spirits to which other flavours have been added. A mixture of wine and brandy is known as a fortified wine; examples are sherry and port.

Question
What is meant by 'other volatile materials present in the original liquids'?

Chapter 3 # Reversible changes

3.1 Reversible and irreversible changes

If some sugar is heated it melts and then turns slowly brown and eventually black. The brown substance is known as caramel, and the caramel cannot be turned back into sugar again. The change is permanent and irreversible – such changes are considered in Chapters 4, 5 and 6. This Chapter is concerned with changes which are **reversible**, where the product can easily be turned back into its original form.

3.2 Melting and boiling

(See also Section 1.2.)

When water is heated some of it evaporates; but most of it goes on getting hotter. However, when the temperature reaches the boiling point, it remains there while all the water evaporates, turning into steam. At the boiling point, both water and steam are present. If we continue heating, more water turns into steam; if we cool the steam then the process is reversed and steam turns into water again. This is known as condensation and is what happens in the second stage of distillation (Section 2.2).

If water is cooled, its temperature drops until the freezing point (0°C) is reached. At this temperature both water and ice are present. if cooling continues, more water turns into ice (the temperature remains at 0°C), but if the mixture is heated the process is reversed and ice turns back into water again. (0°C can of course be referred to as the **melting point** of ice.) Reversible processes can be represented by double arrows $\rightleftharpoons$ and the heating and cooling of water can be represented as:

$$\text{ICE} \underset{}{\overset{0°C}{\rightleftharpoons}} \text{WATER} \underset{}{\overset{100°C}{\rightleftharpoons}} \text{STEAM}$$

Since ice, water and steam are chemically the same substance, in the three different **states of matter**, solid, liquid and gas, we can also represent the change like this:

$$\text{SOLID WATER} \underset{}{\overset{0°C}{\rightleftharpoons}} \text{LIQUID WATER} \underset{}{\overset{100°C}{\rightleftharpoons}} \text{GASEOUS WATER}$$

Almost every substance can exist in each of the three states – solid, liquid or gas – but the melting and boiling points differ for each substance. Some examples are given in Fig 3.1.

The state in which we find a substance depends on the temperature at which we examine it. For example, above 218°C all three of the substances in Fig 3.1 would be gases and below −182°C all would be solids. Normally of course we work at 'room temperature' which is about 20°C. At this temperature water is a liquid, methane is a gas and naphthalene is a solid.

Fig 3.1 Melting and boiling points for three substances

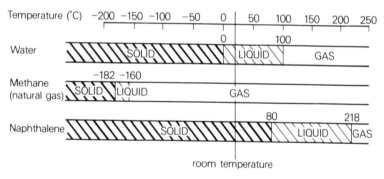

room temperature

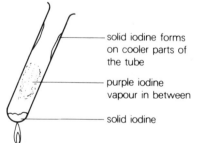

solid iodine forms on cooler parts of the tube

purple iodine vapour in between

solid iodine

Fig 3.2 Sublimation

3.3 Subliming

It is possible for ice to turn straight into a gas without melting. This often happens on cold, clear, winter days. This process of a solid turning directly into a gas is known as **sublimation** and, as in melting and boiling, the change is reversible (Fig 3.2).

Ammonium chloride is a white solid which sublimes when heated and this fascinated the medieval alchemists who knew it as 'sal ammoniac'. Other substances you may meet which sublime are iodine (a purple solid) and 'dry ice' (solid white carbon dioxide which sublimes at $-78°C$).

3.4 Chemical changes

Changes of state such as melting, boiling and subliming are examples of **physical changes** in which the chemical nature of the substance does not alter. For example water and steam are both the same chemical. Again, when wax melts, the liquid produced is still wax, only in a different form, and no new substance has been made.

Changes which result in new chemicals being formed are called **chemical reactions**. Some chemical reactions are reversible and examples are given in the next section.

3.5 Heating copper sulphate and cobalt chloride crystals

When blue copper sulphate crystals are heated in a test-tube they turn white and moisture is seen further up the tube. This liquid can be collected using the apparatus shown in Fig 3.3. The liquid boils at 100°C and it can be shown to be water. If the white solid and test-tube are weighed their mass is found to be less than the mass of blue crystals and test-tube with which we started. We say that the blue crystals have **decomposed** (that is, have been broken down chemically) and have **given off** water.

When the white solid is cooled and water is added to it, the solid becomes warm and turns blue again. The process is reversible and can be written:

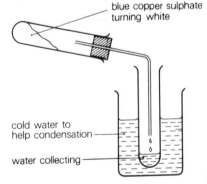

blue copper sulphate turning white

cold water to help condensation

water collecting

Fig 3.3 Heating copper sulphate

$$\text{HYDRATED COPPER SULPHATE (blue)} \underset{}{\overset{\text{heat}}{\rightleftharpoons}} \text{ANHYDROUS COPPER SULPHATE (white)} + \text{WATER}$$

The words **hydrated** and **anhydrous** are based on Greek and mean 'with water' and 'without water'.

Another compound which behaves like copper sulphate is cobalt chloride. The hydrated form consists of red crystals which, when heated, give off water and leave a dark blue solid, anhydrous cobalt chloride. The blue solid turns red again if water is added to it, and a pink-red solution forms on top of the solid. This is another example of a reversible decomposition.

HYDRATED COBALT CHLORIDE $\underset{}{\overset{\text{heat}}{\rightleftharpoons}}$ ANHYDROUS COBALT + WATER
(red) CHLORIDE
  (blue)

3.6 Testing for water

The colour changes described in the last Section can be used to test for the presence of water. One such test involves the addition of anhydrous copper sulphate to a liquid thought to contain water. If the copper sulphate turns blue then water is *present* in the liquid. The test does not prove that the liquid is *pure* water. If only a very small drop of the liquid is available, cobalt chloride paper is used. This paper is pale pink to start with. When it is heated gently, water is driven off and the paper turns blue. This blue paper is placed in the liquid. If it turns pale pink again the liquid contains water.

These tests show only that water is present, and a liquid which gives a positive result may be a mixture of water with some other substance (for example salt solution). To test whether a liquid is pure or is a solution the boiling point must be found. If it boils steadily at or near 100°C* it is pure water. A solution of a solid in water will boil at a temperature *higher* than that of pure water. As the water evaporates and the solution becomes more concentrated, the boiling point will rise.

* The exact value depends on the atmospheric pressure.

Summary

1. Reversible changes are those where the product of the change can easily be turned back to its original form.
2. Changes of state such as melting, freezing, boiling, condensing and subliming are reversible changes.
3. Chemical reactions are changes in which new substances are formed. Some chemical reactions are reversible. Examples are the decomposition of hydrated copper sulphate and hydrated cobalt chloride.
4. The presence of water may be tested using anhydrous copper sulphate (white → blue) or cobalt chloride paper (blue → pink). Pure water may be recognized by its steady boiling point at or near 100°C.

Questions

1.† From the following list of words fill in the blank spaces in the passage:

Blue, green, pink, white, yellow, acid, alcohol, vapour, water, boiled, concentrated, condensed, dissolved, melted.

When red ink is put into a flask and ...., a .... is given off at 100°C. This condenses in the Liebig condenser to give a clear, colourless liquid. When the liquid is mixed with anhydrous cobalt chloride, the cobalt chloride changes colour from .... to .... What is left in the flask is .... red ink. When .... is added to this, normal red ink is again obtained.

2. When hydrated cobalt chloride is heated, it turns blue and water is given off.

a. Draw a diagram of apparatus suitable for heating the cobalt chloride and collecting the water.
b. What test would you do to show that pure water had been given off?
c. How would you discover whether the cobalt chloride gains mass, loses mass or remains the same?
d. What result would you expect in c. and why?
e. What would you do to show that the decomposition is reversible? What would you expect to observe?

3. Which of the following changes are reversible and which are permanent?

a. The melting of naphthalene.
b. The boiling of ethanol.
c. The sublimation of iodine.
d. A candle burning.
e. Salt dissolving in water.
f. The freezing of water.
g. Cobalt chloride paper turning pink.

4. The following results were obtained with four colourless liquids A, B, C and D.

Liquid	Boiling point (°C)	Action on cobalt chloride paper
A	101	stays blue
B	105	turns pink
C	100	turns pink
D	57	stays blue

a. Which of the four is pure water?
b. Which of the four is impure water?
c. Which would turn anhydrous copper sulphate blue?

5.

a. Explain to a younger brother, who has done no science, the difference between melting and dissolving.
b. Your mother claims that when sugar is added to a cup of *hot* tea, it melts. How would you try to discover whether she is right?

6. Write sentences which include each of the following words. You may include more than one of the words in the same sentence. The sentence should convey some idea of the meaning of the word.
Sublime, hydrated, decompose, distil, solvent, anhydrous, reversible.

31

7.[†] Blue crystals of copper sulphate appear to be quite dry, but when they are heated water vapour is given off and they lose mass. The residue left after heating is a white powder. When water is added drop by drop to this white powder, the water is absorbed and the powder gets quite hot.

In order to find what proportion of the crystals consists of water, a weighed sample was heated in a crucible. The results were:

Mass of crucible	= 14.20 g
Mass of crucible + copper sulphate crystals	= 19.20 g
Mass of crucible + white powder after heating	= 17.40 g

a. Find the mass of water in 100 g of the crystals as follows:
 i Work out the mass of copper sulphate crystals.
 ii Work out the mass of water in the crystals.
 iii Work out the mass of water in 100 g of crystals.
b. If you were doing this experiment, how would you know that the copper sulphate had been heated for long enough to drive out all the water?
c. Why did the white powder get hot when water was added to it?
d. A boy doing the experiment was impressed by the amount of heat given out and suggested that this might be a useful method of producing heat energy. What do you think of this suggestion?

Chapter 4 **Permanent changes**

In Chapter 3 we looked at various changes which all had one thing in common: they were reversible. (These changes are sometimes called 'temporary'.) In this Chapter we are concerned with changes which cannot easily be reversed. These are known as **permanent** changes.

Before substances are heated they are weighed and after heating the residue which remains is weighed. There are three possibilities: a gain in mass, no change in mass, or a loss in mass. Where no difference of mass is recorded the substance has not changed chemically (but a physical change may have occurred, as for example when ice turns into water). If there is a gain in mass this is always due to the air, part of which has combined with the substance. Such changes are considered at the end of this Chapter (Section 4.5) and in Chapter 5.

What happens when mass is lost? Has matter been destroyed? If we look into these situations more carefully we find that a gas has been given off, and we can show this by collecting it. It is not an easy job to weigh gases, but when this is done, it is found that the mass of the gas makes up for the mass lost by the substance which was heated:

SUBSTANCE $\longrightarrow$ SOLID RESIDUE $+$ GAS
mass m $\qquad$ mass $m-x$ $\qquad$ mass x

4.1 Loss of water

When a substance is heated one gas which may be given off is steam, which can be easily condensed back to water. Section 3.5 dealt with the loss of water from two *hydrated* salts: copper sulphate and cobalt chloride. If all the water had been condensed and weighed, it would have just made up for the mass lost by the crystals when they were heated.

In these cases the loss of water was *reversible*, but not all compounds which lose water do so reversibly. For example, purple crystals of chrome alum lose water (which can be tested in the usual way) leaving a green solid. Addition of water to this green solid does not result in the purple crystals forming again. This is an example of a *permanent* change.

4.2 Loss of oxygen

If substances like potassium permanganate or red lead oxide are heated they lose mass. Any attempt to condense the gas (using the apparatus shown in Fig 3.3) would fail because the gas being given off is oxygen, not steam. The oxygen can be collected by making it displace water from a test-tube (Fig 4.1). The tubes used to collect the gas are filled with water and left upside down until they are needed. The oxygen which is given off forces its way through the apparatus and fills the collecting tube. Full tubes are corked under the surface of the water. The first tube will contain a mixture of oxygen and air, because air is pushed out of the apparatus by the oxygen. If the volume of oxygen is to be measured, a gas syringe may be used instead of the collecting tube (Fig 4.2). If no gas syringe is available, a graduated tube (marked with volume) can be used instead of the test-tube shown in Fig 4.1.*

The chemical test for oxygen is that it will 'rekindle a glowing splint'. A **splint** is a thin piece of wood. This is lit

*A more convenient laboratory preparation of oxygen is described in Appendix 2.

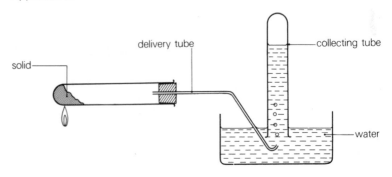

Fig 4.1 Collecting oxygen over water

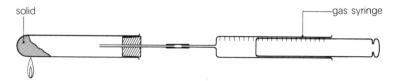

Fig 4.2 Measuring the volume of gas given off when a solid is heated

and blown out so that it glows; then, if it is placed in oxygen it catches fire again (rekindles). The gas in the collecting tubes may be tested in this way, or the glowing splint may be rekindled at the mouth of the tube in which the gas is being prepared. Sometimes the rekindling makes a slight noise, which should not be confused with the 'squeaky pop' in the test for hydrogen.

4.3 Loss of carbon dioxide

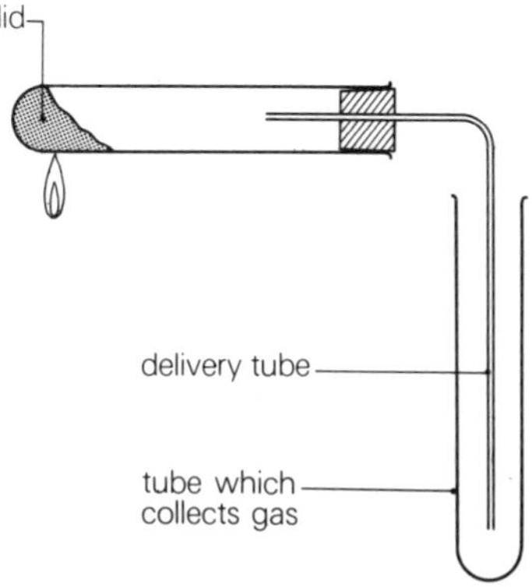

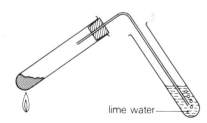

Fig 4.3 Collecting carbon dioxide (denser than air)

When some compounds, known as carbonates (for example copper carbonate) are heated, they give off a gas called carbon dioxide. (As it does this, copper carbonate turns from green to black.) The gas may be collected 'over water' as in Fig 4.1, but this is not very satisfactory because some of the carbon dioxide dissolves in the water. As it is heavier (denser) than air it can be collected in the apparatus shown in Fig 4.3

Carbon dioxide is usually recognized by its property of turning limewater milky. (Limewater is calcium hydroxide solution and the milkiness is a fine suspension of calcium carbonate particles.) To test whether the gas is being given off from a reaction in a test-tube, the apparatus in Fig. 4.4 can be used, with the delivery tube dipping under the surface of limewater in the right-hand test-tube. Alternatively a teat pipette can be placed as in Fig 4.5a. The bulb is squeezed several times to fill the pipette with the gas which is then blown out through limewater (Fig 4.5b). If a test-tube of carbon dioxide is to be tested, some limewater can simply be added and the tube shaken. It is important not to use too much limewater since otherwise the milkiness will take a long time to appear. Another problem can be that the milkiness disappears if too much carbon dioxide is present,

Fig 4.4 Testing for carbon dioxide (method 1)

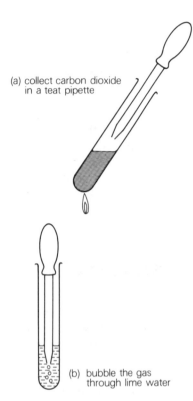

(a) collect carbon dioxide in a teat pipette

(b) bubble the gas through lime water

Fig 4.5 Testing for carbon dioxide (method 2)

but this is only a difficulty if the experiment is left and not watched.

4.4 Heating sulphur

When sulphur is heated in a crucible which is open to the air, a blue flame is seen and the solid disappears leaving no trace except for a sharp smell. Does this mean that the sulphur is decomposing like the substances described above? The question can be answered by heating sulphur in the absence of air. (This can be done by heating sulphur in a test-tube, the sulphur gas which is given off pushes the air out of the tube before the sulphur is hot enough to catch fire.) The sulphur melts, then turns into a thick, black substance and finally boils. It does not decompose and therefore the original disappearance of the sulphur had something to do with the air. In fact the sulphur has **reacted** with part of the air to form a gas, as we shall see in the next Chapter.

4.5 Heating magnesium and copper

When a piece of magnesium is heated in air, it will eventually flare up and burn with a brilliant white flame leaving a white ash behind. If this reaction is carried out in a crucible (with a lid to stop the ash escaping) it is found that the ash weighs more than the magnesium did. Something has been taken from the air and has increased the mass of the magnesium, changing it into a new substance.

Another experiment is to fold up a piece of copper foil, hold it in tongs, and heat it in air. This reaction is much less spectacular than the heating of magnesium. The copper becomes coated with a black layer on the outside and there is a slight increase in mass. When the foil is unfolded, the copper which was not in contact with the air is shiny, not blackened. This shows that the air was responsible for the blackening. The copper has reacted with part of the air. A more complicated experiment is to heat copper in a vacuum.

Then it remains shiny and its mass does not change.

Both these reactions are discussed again in the next Chapter.

Summary

1. Permanent changes are those which are not easily reversed.

2.

Change of mass on heating a substance	What has occurred?
none	no change at all or a physical change only (e.g. melting)
loss	gas given off
gain	substance has reacted with part of the air

3. Common gases which are given off when solids decompose are:
   steam (test – condenses back to water);
   oxygen (test – rekindles a glowing splint);
   carbon dioxide (test – turns limewater milky).

Questions

1. 4.99 g of the purple solid chrome alum are heated. Water is given off and the solid turns green. Heating is continued until no more water comes off. The green solid is found to weigh 2.83 g.

a. Sketch an apparatus that you could use to collect the water which is given off.

b. How would you prove that the liquid you collected was water?

c. What mass of water would you expect to be given off?

d. When water is added to the green solid, it stays green. Do you think that the solid is anhydrous chrome alum or do you think that there has been a permanent chemical change?

2. When zinc carbonate is heated, it gives off carb
dioxide.
a. How would you show that the gas is carbon dioxide?
b. What change in mass would you expect if the solid h
been weighed before and after heating?

3.
a. How would you prepare three test-tubes of pu
oxygen?
b. How would you show that the gas is oxygen?
c. Potassium permanganate gives off oxygen when it
heated. What happens to the mass of the solid as it
heated?

4.[†] Three different solids A, B, C behave as follows wh
heated:
A melts, but does not decompose or vaporize;
B gives off oxygen gas;
C gives off some water vapour, but suffers no furth
change.
a. State in each case what changes in mass you wou
expect (gain, loss or no change) when the solids A,
and C are heated.
b. Explain how it is possible for a substance to gain ma
when heated in air.
c. Name one substance which does gain in mass wh
heated in air.

5. When washing soda crystals are heated, steam a
carbon dioxide are given off.
a. Draw a labelled diagram of an apparatus you could use
heat the crystals and to try to collect both water a
carbon dioxide.
b. Give a test (and its result) for:
i Water.
ii Carbon dioxide.

6.[†] The manufacturers of a certain washing powder cla
that when it is placed in boiling water oxygen is given c
a. Give a labelled sketch of the apparatus you could use
test this claim and collect the gas given off.
b. How would you test that the gas was oxygen?

7.[†] The apparatus shown in the diagram (Fig 4.6) was used for heating various solids:

a. Before heating, the syringe was half full of air. After heating for about five minutes, the apparatus was cooled back to room temperature, and the change in the volume of gas in the syringe was observed. The whole experiment was done four times using the four solids listed below, and starting with fresh apparatus each time. For each case, state what happened to the volume of gas in the syringe as a result of heating the solid:

   i Copper foil.

   ii Dry sand.

   iii *Either* red lead oxide *or* potassium permanganate.

   iv Copper sulphate crystals.

b. In cases i and iv above, what would you *see* happening to the solid while it was being heated?

c. In cases i and iii above, what would happen to the mass of the solid? Explain your answers briefly.

Fig 4.6

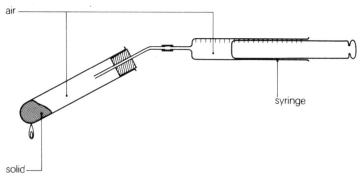

8. (Difficult)

Can you suggest reasons why:

a. A little limewater goes milky very quickly when carbon dioxide is passed into it, but a large amount of limewater tends to stay transparent for some time before the milkiness appears.

b. A little limewater goes milky and then clear again if a lot of carbon dioxide is passed into it.

c. Fizzy drinks (which contain dissolved carbon dioxide) tend more often to come frothing out of a newly opened bottle in summer than in winter.

9.[†] The following is the laboratory record of a boy who had been finding out what happened when certain solids were heated in air.

Name of solid	Colour before heating	Colour during heating	Colour after heating	Mass change of solid	Effect of adding water to cold residue
cobalt chloride	red	blue	blue	loss	dissolves to give red solution
zinc oxide	white	yellow	white	none	does not dissolve
nickel carbonate	green	black	black	loss	does not dissolve
potassium chloride	white	white	white	none	dissolves to give colourless solution
iron wire	grey	red hot	black	gain	does not dissolve

On the evidence provided in the table:
a. Which of the substances were affected by the heating?
b. Which substance was temporarily affected during the time it was being heated?
c. Is potassium chloride soluble in water? Justify your answer.
d. Where could the increase in mass of the iron wire have come from?
e. On the evidence above, is it possible to say whether or not nickel carbonate is soluble in water?
f. What substance could have been the cause of the loss in mass when cobalt chloride was heated?

10. Opposite are three statements about heating substances. They are correct, but the reasons given are not. In each case:
   i Describe simple experiments you could do to show that the reason given is wrong.
   ii Write out the correct reason.

	Statement	Incorrect reason
a.	Potassium permanganate loses mass when heated	part of it is destroyed
b.	Copper turns black when heated in air	the bunsen flame deposits soot on it
c.	Copper sulphate crystals give off water on heating	they must have been damp to start with

Background reading

Weighing experiments
When copper sulphate is heated it loses mass, as you know. The masses before and after heating can be found using three weighings:
mass of empty test-tube,
mass of test-tube plus blue copper sulphate crystals before heating,
mass of test-tube plus white anhydrous copper sulphate after heating.
The masses of copper sulphate before and after heating can be calculated by subtracting the mass of the test-tube from the second and third weighings.

If 5 g of copper sulphate crystals are heated, 3.2 g of anhydrous solid are left. If 10 g of copper sulphate are heated, 6.4 g of anhydrous solid would be expected, and if 2.5 g are heated, 1.6 g of solid. We say that these results are **in proportion**.

Plotting graphs
If all the members of your class heat copper sulphate, weighing the tube before and after the experiment, you can present their results on a graph, plotting *mass of anhydrous copper sulphate* against *mass of hydrated copper sulphate*. If the results are in proportion (as they should be) they will lie on a straight line that passes through the origin, as shown in Fig 4.7.

When plotting any graph it is a good idea to do it in a series of steps.

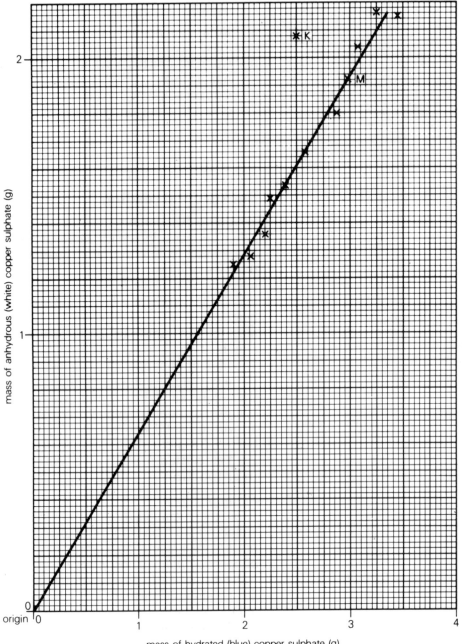

Fig 4.7

1. Choose the scales in order to make the best use of the paper. Look for the greatest value of each of the two things you are plotting. This will tell you the largest number you need on each axis. Then pick a scale from which you can easily read values : for example, let one big square on the graph paper be 1 g, 2 g or 5 g, (or 0.1 g, 0.2 g, 0.5 g) but not 3 g or 6 g (or 0.3 g, 0.6 g) and certainly not $3\frac{1}{2}$ g.*
2. Label each axis clearly and include the units.
3. Plot the points carefully, using small crosses.
4. Decide whether the line should go through the origin. In this case if no copper sulphate is heated, no solid will be left, so the line should go through the origin.
5. Decide whether any of the points don't fit. In this example point K was obtained by a boy who was late for the lesson and did not finish.
6. Decide whether a straight line or a curve best fits the points. Do not join all the points.
7. Draw the line. If it is straight it is called the **best straight line** through the points, and a transparent ruler is very useful to help you draw it. Because of experimental error not all the points lie on the line. It is impossible to weigh with complete accuracy and this causes a 'scatter' of points around the line, but they should average out with about the same number of points on either side of the line.

All decomposition reactions obey the same rules. If *mass of residue* is plotted against *mass heated* we shall always get a straight line through the origin.

Gas densities

Density measures the mass of a 'unit volume'. In our usual units this means it is the mass in grams of one cubic centimetre (cm^3) of substance. For example, each of the small cubes in Fig 4.8 has a volume of 1 cm^3. If the whole lump weighs 20 g, then the mass of 1 $cm^3 = \dfrac{20}{5} = 4$ g. We say that the density is 'four grams per cubic centimetre'

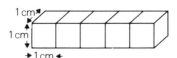

Fig 4.8 5 cubes, each of volume 1 cm^3

* The figures for the variables *you* decide (not the ones that are produced by the experiment) must always be plotted on the horizontal axis (*x*-axis).

which we write as 4 g/cm³. So:

$$\text{DENSITY} = \frac{\text{MASS}}{\text{VOLUME}}$$

Six 1 cm³ cubes of the same substance will weigh 24 g and the density is

$$\frac{\text{mass}}{\text{volume}} = \frac{24}{6} = 4 \, \text{g/cm}^3,$$

the same as before, because it is the same substance. An *irregular lump* of substance with volume 8 cm³ will weigh 32 g and so its density will still be 4 g/cm³.

To measure the density of a gas we need to know the *mass* of a certain *volume*. We can measure the volume in a gas syringe or graduated tube, but weighing gases is difficult. However, if the gas is given off when a solid decomposes, we know that the *mass of the gas* is equal to the *mass lost by the solid*. Thus if the solid lost 0.1 g and the volume of the gas was 100 cm³, the density of the gas would be:

$$\frac{\text{mass}}{\text{volume}} = \frac{0.1}{100} = 0.001 \, \text{g/cm}^3.$$

Consider an example from an experiment where potassium permanganate is heated, giving off oxygen (using the apparatus shown in Fig 4.9).

Mass of potassium permanganate before heating	= 2.63 g
Mass of residue after heating	= 2.52 g
Mass loss	= 0.11 g
Volume of gas in syringe at start	= 2 cm³
Volume of gas in syringe after heating	= 84 cm³
Volume of oxygen	= 82 cm³
(Room temperature 20°C)	

This means that 82 cm³ of oxygen weigh 0.11 g. The mass of 1 cm³ is given by:

$$\frac{\text{mass}}{\text{volume}} = \frac{0.11}{82} = 0.0013 \, \text{g/cm}^3.$$

Since this number is so small, it is usually expressed in grams per litre (dm³); a litre is a thousand times as big as one cubic centimetre, so 1 litre of oxygen will weigh one thousand times as much.

$0.0013 \times 1000 = 1.3 \, \text{g/dm}^3$ at 20°C

solid — gas syringe

Fig. 4.9 Heating potassium permanganate

Gases expand when they are heated, so the temperature at which the measurement was made should also be given.

The second example is from an experiment where zinc carbonate gives off carbon dioxide when it is heated.

Mass of zinc carbonate before heating = 4.97 g
Mass of residue after heating   = 4.80 g
Mass of carbon dioxide   = 0.17 g
Volume in syringe at the start   =   3 cm³
Volume in syringe after heating   = 96 cm³
Volume of carbon dioxide   = 93 cm³
(Room temperature 25 °C)

Thus the density of carbon dioxide $= \dfrac{0.17}{93}$

$= 0.0018 \, g/cm^3$
$= 1.8 \, g/dm^3$ at 25 °C

Since the amount of gas given off is *proportional* to the loss of mass, several experiments can be carried out and a graph plotted to make sure that the errors are small. For example, Fig 4.10 shows a graph obtained by plotting *loss of mass* against *volume of oxygen*, for a number of experiments where potassium permanganate was heated. To work out the density we could take any point on the graph and divide the mass of the gas by the volume it occupies. For example point A, density $= \dfrac{0.06}{46}$; point B, density $= \dfrac{0.09}{70}$. But to make the division sum easy, a convenient volume, for example 100 cm³, can be used. The corresponding loss of mass can be read from the graph (0.13 g) even though no experiment gave as much as 100 cm³ of gas. The calculation is now:

density of oxygen $= \dfrac{mass}{volume} = \dfrac{0.13}{100} = 0.0013 \, g/cm^3$ at 20 °C.

Measuring and errors
Even when a lot of care is taken, it is still impossible to avoid small errors when making measurements. When weighing it

45

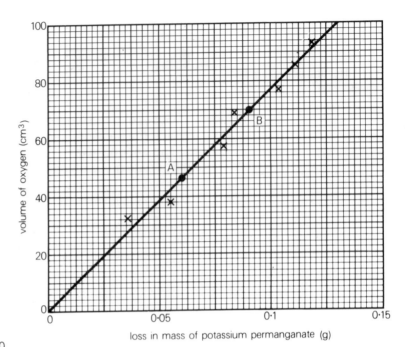

Fig 4.10

is often difficult to be more accurate than 0.01 g (this depends on the type of balance used). This does not matter much in a mass of 5.00 g, but it matters more if you are 0.01 g wrong when the value is 0.13 g as in the last example.

Gas volumes are measured in gas syringes. Here it is difficult to be more accurate than about 1 or 2 cm³. Again, this is not too important in a value of 90 cm³, but it makes a big difference if the value is only 10 cm³. A measuring cylinder (used to measure volumes of liquid) can be read to similar accuracy.

Errors of this sort tend to be *random*, that is, the values are sometimes too high and sometimes too low. If we do an experiment enough times (as happens when a class 'pools' its results) then the high and low values tend to cancel each other out and we get a more reliable answer.

It is valuable to plot a graph, because this shows which values are really wrong (for example point K in Fig 4.7) and which values cannot be avoided because the apparatus is not perfect. Also, a point on the line is more accurate than any individual result, because the line represents the average of the results.

Questions
1. Look at the graph in Fig. 4.7 and at number 5 in the steps for plotting graphs on page 43 and explain why the point K occurs above the line, and not on it.
2. The density of hydrogen at 25°C is 0.08 g/dm³ and the density of nitrogen at the same temperature is 1.2 g/dm³.
a. What are the masses of the following at 25°C?
 i 1 cm³ of hydrogen.
 ii 100 cm³ of hydrogen.
 iii 1 cm³ of nitrogen.
 iv 54 cm³ of nitrogen.
b. What are the volumes (at 25°C) of:
 i 8 g of hydrogen?
 ii 1 g of hydrogen?
 iii 12 g of nitrogen?
 iv 0.5 g of nitrogen?
c. What volume of hydrogen will have the same mass as 100 cm³ of nitrogen?

3. Six pairs of pupils heated some blue copper sulphate crystals in identical test-tubes. The crystals turned white and were found to lose mass. The pupils obtained the results below.

Mass of tube and blue crystals before heating (grams)	Mass of tube and white powder after heating (grams)
17.51	16.60
16.02	15.65
16.40	15.85
16.85	16.61
15.64	15.40
17.10	16.34

a. Plot a graph of *mass of tube and contents before heating* against *loss in mass* showing loss in mass on the vertical axis.

b. Which group would you advise to repeat the experiment?
c. What do you think was the probable cause of their error?
d. Use the graph to work out the mass of the test-tube.
e. Use the graph to work out the mass of white copper sulphate that could be obtained by heating 1 gram of the blue crystals.

4. All the members of a class heated samples of red lead oxide and measured the volume of oxygen evolved. Their results were:

Mass of tube and contents before heating (g)	Mass of tube and contents after heating (g)	Volume of oxygen (cm^3)
6.31	5.21	870
10.62	9.42	700
5.43	4.55	630
2.52	2.18	260
8.46	7.93	370
3.97	3.23	560
8.76	7.51	960

a. Plot a graph of *loss in mass* of the lead oxide (on the horizontal axis) against volume of oxygen.
b. Which of the points is obviously wrong? Three members of the class suggested reasons for this inaccurate result:
   i Too much red lead was taken and thus it did not all decompose.
   ii There was a leak in the syringe.
   iii The syringe was not at zero to start with.
   Consider each of these in turn and state why it could or could not have caused the inaccuracy.
c. What mass would be lost in an experiment in which 100 cm^3 of gas was obtained?
d. Work out a value for the density of oxygen at the temperature of the experiment:
   i In grams per cm^3.
   ii In grams per litre.

5.† A pupil heats some red lead oxide in a test-tube and collects the gas given off in a syringe. During the course of the heating the test-tube is weighed and the volume of oxygen given off noted.

Time (min.)	Mass of the test-tube (g)	Volume of oxygen (cm³)
0	8.56	0
1	8.53	25
2	8.48	60
3	8.44	90
4	8.44	90
5	8.44	90

a. Plot a graph to show how the mass changes with time.
b. How long does it take for all the red lead oxide to decompose?
c. How can the pupil be sure that all the red lead has decomposed at the end of the experiment?
d. From the figures, calculate the density of oxygen in g/cm³.

Chapter 5 **Burning and oxidation**

At the end of the last Chapter we saw that the disappearance of sulphur and the gain in mass of magnesium and copper when heated had something to do with the air. We must therefore know something about the air before we can explain what happened.

5.1 The air

The air is a mixture of gases which can be separated by fractional distillation (Section 2.5). The most abundant (commonest) gas in the air is the unreactive gas nitrogen which accounts for 78% (just under $\frac{4}{5}$) of the air. The next most common is oxygen (Section 4.2) which accounts for 20% (about $\frac{1}{5}$) of the air. Then there is argon (about 1%) together with even less of helium, neon, krypton and xenon. These five gases are very unreactive and are known as the noble (or inert) gases. Fig 5.1 shows the composition of air in a **pie chart**. The air contains water vapour and carbon dioxide (Section 4.3), but the quantities of these vary and they are never more than a very small percentage of the air.

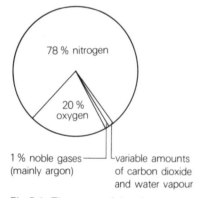

78 % nitrogen

20 % oxygen

1 % noble gases (mainly argon)

variable amounts of carbon dioxide and water vapour

Fig 5.1 The gases of the air

5.2 Oxygen and burning

Oxygen is the most reactive gas in the air. When a substance is heated in air and gains mass, it is therefore more likely to have reacted with the oxygen than with anything else. Evidence for this comes from several experiments:
1. We saw in the last Chapter that when a folded piece of copper is heated the parts in contact with the air blacken. However, when a piece of copper is heated in nitrogen

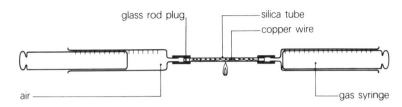

Fig 5.2 Measuring the volume change when air is passed over heated copper

(or in air from which the oxygen has been removed) it remains unaffected.

2. An important experiment uses the apparatus shown in Fig 5.2. Using syringes, air is passed over heated copper which is contained in a thin silica tube. The copper turns black and, as it does so, the volume of air decreases. However, when about $\frac{1}{5}$ of the air has been used up, there is no further change in volume. If some of the unreacted copper is heated it does not turn black. These observations suggest that it is the oxygen in the air which is used. This can be confirmed by disconnecting the apparatus and expelling the gas from one of the syringes. At the same time a glowing splint is placed near the nozzle of the syringe. The splint will go out; if the syringe had contained any oxygen the splint would have continued to glow.

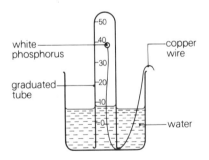

Fig 5.3 Measuring the volume change when phosphorus burns in air

3. A similar experiment uses phosphorus, which is a substance that smoulders in air. Using the apparatus in Fig 5.3 it can be shown that only $\frac{1}{5}$ of the air is used up before the reaction stops and that the gas which remains will put out a burning splint. **This experiment should be done only by your teacher. Phosphorus is a dangerous substance which must be stored under water since it catches fire in air.**

4. Substances burn more vigorously in pure oxygen than they do in air.

So it is the oxygen in the air which is the active part. Nitrogen will react with other substances only at extremely high temperatures and the noble gases do not combine at all.

5.3 The formation of oxides

All these reactions produce a new substance. The original

substance **combines** with the oxygen to form an **oxide**:

MAGNESIUM + OXYGEN ⟶ MAGNESIUM OXIDE (see Section 4.5)
COPPER + OXYGEN ⟶ COPPER OXIDE (see Section 4.5)
PHOSPHORUS + OXYGEN ⟶ PHOSPHORUS OXIDE

Such reaction with oxygen is known as **oxidation**.

These oxidation reactions are also also known as **burning** or **combustion** and the oxides produced are called the **combustion products**.

5.4 Oxides of sulphur and carbon

While the oxides of magnesium, copper and phosphorus are all solids at room temperature, those of sulphur and carbon are gases. This explains why sulphur apparently disappears when it is heated in air, as we saw in Section 4.4. What happens is that the sulphur melts and then burns in air to form the new substance, sulphur dioxide (the *di*- here means 'two' – as also in carbon *di*oxide). The sulphur dioxide (which is responsible for the sharp smell) then mixes with the other gases in the air. The sulphur dioxide weighs more than the sulphur and this can be demonstrated if an apparatus similar to that of Fig 5.7 is used. A known mass of sulphur is burned and the gas is absorbed in soda lime. (The soda lime 'sucks up' the gas rather like a sponge sucking up water.) The increase in mass of the soda lime tubes gives the mass of the sulphur dioxide.

Carbon behaves in the same way. When it is burned it forms carbon dioxide, which can be detected by using limewater. Once again the carbon apparently disappears, though if wood charcoal is used a little ash remains because wood charcoal is not a pure form of carbon.

5.5 The burning of compounds

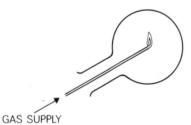

GAS SUPPLY

Fig 5.4 Burning natural gas in a flask

If natural gas (methane) is burned in a flask (Fig 5.4) *two*

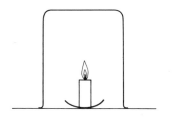

Fig 5.5 Burning a candle under a beaker

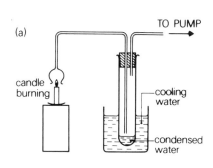

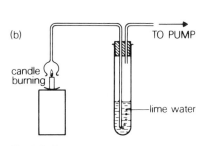

Fig 5.6 Detecting water and carbon dioxide in the products of combustion of a candle

products of burning can be identified. One product is the condensation on the inside of the flask; this turns blue cobalt chloride pink and is therefore water. Water is the oxide of hydrogen ('hydrogen' means 'water former'). The flask can also be shown to contain carbon dioxide by shaking some limewater in it. We can therefore write:

METHANE + OXYGEN ⟶ CARBON DIOXIDE + HYDROGEN OXIDE
(water)

It is thus reasonable to say that methane contains some carbon and some hydrogen. If it were a *mixture* of the two we should see little specks of carbon. We cannot because the carbon and hydrogen are chemically combined and are called a **compound.**

Carbon and hydrogen are called **elements** as they cannot be broken down into simpler substances. We can recognize elements when we burn them because they give *one oxide only.* Compounds, which consist of two or more elements combined together, usually give the oxides of those elements when they burn. You will find out more about elements in Chapter 8.

Candle wax is another example of a compound. When a lighted candle is placed under a beaker (Fig 5.5) it goes out when it has used all the oxygen in the air. Water (condensation) and carbon dioxide are produced. Experiments which show this are illustrated in Fig 5.6. In Fig 5.6a water condenses in the tube and can be tested by using cobalt chloride paper. In Fig 5.6b the limewater turns milky showing the presence of carbon dioxide.

The apparatus shown in Fig 5.6 can also be used to show that alcohol (ethanol) gives carbon dioxide and water when it burns. Thus it must contain carbon and hydrogen. In fact it also contains oxygen, but it is not possible to tell this by looking at the products of burning which get some of their oxygen from the air.

Not all elements react directly with the air to form their oxides and neither do all compounds burn in air. Many compounds containing carbon burn, but there are important exceptions such as carbon tetrachloride (tetrachloro-methane) and trichloroethane (a dry-cleaning solvent).

Some carbon compounds which do burn in air are useful

as **fuels**, since they are available in large quantities and give a lot of heat when they burn. An important group of compounds are the **hydrocarbons**, which are compounds of just hydrogen and carbon as the name suggests. Examples are methane (natural gas), propane, butane (calor gas), octane (one substance in car petrol) and benzene. These all give carbon dioxide and water when they burn.

When a compound burns, the products of combustion tell us something of the elements contained in the compound. For example, hydrocarbons burn to give carbon dioxide and water, and carbon disulphide burns to give carbon dioxide and sulphur dioxide. However, ethanol (which also contains oxygen) burns to give carbon dioxide and water, so it is not possible to identify all the elements (especially oxygen) from the combustion products.

5.6 Changes in mass on burning

When substances burn, they take in oxygen from the air and gain in mass. This is not at all obvious when ethanol is burned in a crucible for the ethanol disappears completely. However, if the apparatus shown in Fig 5.7 is used, the water and the carbon dioxide produced can be absorbed in the solid called soda lime. The mass of ethanol burned can be measured by weighing the crucible at the beginning and end of the experiment. The U-tubes are also weighed before and after the experiment and their increase in mass is found to be greater than the mass of ethanol burned. We have assumed that the carbon dioxide and water trapped by the soda lime all came from the burned ethanol. However, some of it might have come from the air and would have been sucked in whether we were burning ethanol or not. To test this we carry out what is called a **control experiment**. In this air is drawn through the apparatus for the same length of time as the ethanol took to burn. The U-tubes *do* gain in mass slightly, showing that some carbon dioxide and water vapour did come from the air. The gain in mass of the U-tubes in this experiment must be subtracted from the gain

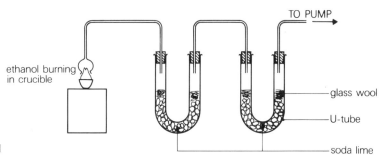

TO PUMP

ethanol burning
in crucible

glass wool

U-tube

soda lime

Fig 5.7 Collecting and weighing
the products of combustion of ethanol

which was noticed when the ethanol was burned. However, it is still found that the carbon dioxide and water vapour produced by the burning ethanol weigh more than the ethanol did to start with.

This experiment can also be used to investigate the burning of a candle or sulphur (Section 5.4). Once again it is found that the oxides weigh more than the substance which was burned.

5.7 Breathing

Breathing is a process very similar to burning. Just as burning uses oxygen, so does breathing. A burning candle produces heat because of the oxidation reaction which takes place. The oxygen we breathe oxidises the foodstuffs we eat and the reaction produces the energy that we need. Carbohydrates contain carbon and hydrogen (as the name suggests) and also oxygen. They are oxidized to carbon dioxide and water. We breathe these out. We also breathe out the unreactive gases which our bodies did not want and any oxygen which has not been used up.

5.8 Rusting

Steel (a form of iron) is one of the cheapest and most useful metals, but its greatest disadvantage is the fact that it reacts with the gases of the air to form rust. Chemists need to know as much as possible about the process of rusting so they can try to prevent it.

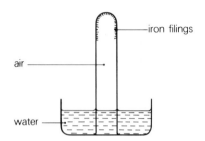

iron filings

air

water

Fig 5.8 The rusting of iron

Which parts of the air cause rusting? From our experience we might well suggest that oxygen is involved. If the experiment shown in Fig 5.8 is set up and left for several days, it is found that about $\frac{1}{5}$ of the air has been used up. The gas remaining in the tube puts out a lighted splint. Therefore oxygen is involved when iron rusts.

However, the air in Fig 5.8 will be moist, so perhaps water vapour is involved as well. We need to set up a series of experiments in which iron is in contact with ordinary (damp) air, dry air and water without air. The last of these is not as simple as it sounds since air is slightly soluble in water. So we need to boil the water to remove dissolved air and then cover it (for example with a layer of grease) to keep the air out. To remove the water from the air we use calcium chloride. So if three test-tubes are set up as in Fig 5.9 it is found that only the iron in tube A rusts, not that in B or C. Thus we can say that both oxygen *and* water are necessary before iron will rust. Investigation of rust shows that it is hydrated iron oxide.

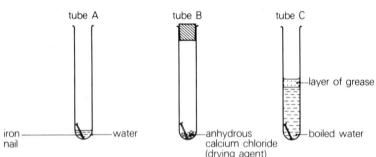

Fig 5.9 Investigating the rusting of iron

The prevention of rusting is a problem which has not been completely solved. Methods of keeping air and moisture away from iron by painting or by turning the surface into iron phosphate are reasonably good. Galvanizing (covering the iron with a layer of zinc) is better as it prevents rusting (even at scratches) by an electrical effect. (See also Section 13.5.)

Summary

1. The air consists of nitrogen (78%), oxygen (20%), noble

gases (1%), carbon dioxide and water vapour (variable amounts).

2. Oxygen is the *active part* of the air. When substances burn in air they *combine* with oxygen to form their *oxides*. These are called *combustion products*.

3. *Elements* (which cannot be broken down to any simpler substance) burn to give single oxides.

4. *Compounds* consist of two or more elements **chemically combined** together. Those which burn usually give a mixture of the oxides of the elements which they contain.

5. When substances burn they gain in mass. If the oxides are gases they must be **absorbed** in a solid (for example soda lime) before they can be weighed.

6. We breathe in oxygen, part of which oxidizes carbon compounds from our food. Thus we breathe out more carbon dioxide than we breathe in.

7. Both water and oxygen are necessary before iron will rust.

Questions

1.†
a. The following substances are all gases. For each gas write 'yes' if you think that the gas is present in the air of the room in which you are sitting, and 'no' if you think it is not.
   Nitrogen, hydrogen, carbon dioxide, water vapour.
b. What would be one effect you would notice if the amount of oxygen in the air were suddenly doubled?

2.
a. What happens to the mass of a piece of copper which is heated in air?
b. Why does this happen?
c. What happens to the mass of a piece of copper which is heated in nitrogen?

3. A piece of phosphorus burns slowly in air at room temperature.
a. How rapidly would phosphorus burn in nitrogen?
b. How rapidly would phosphorus burn in argon?
c. How rapidly would phosphorus burn in oxygen?
d. What is formed when phosphorus burns?

4. Explain why:

a. When a piece of copper is folded and then heated in air, *only* the outside turns black.

b. When alcohol burns, nothing seems to be left at the end.

c. People are advised to roll themselves in a rug (or laboratory fire blanket) if their clothes catch fire.

d. During a fire, doors should be closed.

e. When iron rusts in a limited volume of air, rusting stops when 20% of the air has been used up.

f. When coal is burned, the ash weighs less than the coal; when magnesium burns, the ash weighs more than the magnesium.

5.† Strontium metal burns in air to form a white powder which weighs more than the strontium.

  i What is the chemical name of the powder?

  ii Why does it weigh more than the strontium?

6.† A weighed coil of magnesium ribbon was heated in a crucible, which had its lid resting loosely on it. Although a little smoke was given off as the bottom of the crucible began to glow, it soon stopped coming off. Even when the lid was lifted slightly, no smoke appeared but the coil, now covered in white powder, appeared to glow more brightly. When they were cold the crucible and its contents were weighed again.

a. What was the white powder covering the coil?

b. What was the smoke?

c. Why did the glow grow brighter when the lid was slightly lifted?

d. If the crucible and its contents weighed more at the end of the experiment than they did before being heated, to what conclusion would you come?

e. Why was the lid used?

7. Phosphorus is a dangerous element which will burn of its own accord in air forming a solid compound. A piece of phosphorus was supported in a graduated tube filled with air, as shown in Fig 5.3. The level of the water in the tube started at 0 but when the phosphorus began to smoulder it gradually rose up the tube to the 10 mark and then stopped.

a. What chemical reaction is taking place when the phosphorus begins to smoulder?
b. Why did the water level in the tube rise?
c. Why did the water level stop rising when it reached the 10 mark?
d. The gas left in the tube put out a lighted splint. What was this gas?
e. What does this experiment tell us about the proportion of the different gases in the air?

8. When phosphorus is burned in a flask which has been sealed with a bung, there is no change in the mass of the flask and its contents until the bung is removed.
a. Explain why the mass does not alter until the bung is removed.
b. Would you expect the mass of the flask, bung and contents to increase or decrease as the flask was opened?
c. What might you observe as the bung was removed?

9. A tube containing copper was weighed. Using two syringes, 50 cm³ of air was passed backwards and forwards over the heated copper until the volume did not alter any more. Some of the copper was unchanged. After cooling, the gas volume was measured and the tube was weighed again.
a. Would the tube and copper have gained or lost mass?
b. What has happened to the copper?
c. What would you expect the volume of gas to be after cooling?
d. What was left in the syringes at the end of the experiment?
e. What differences in your readings (mass and volume) would you expect if a greater mass of copper had been used?
f. Roughly what final volume would you expect if you had blown 50 cm³ from your lungs into the apparatus rather than taking 50 cm³ from the room?
g. What final volume would you expect if the syringes had contained a mixture of 10 cm³ oxygen and 10 cm³ nitrogen to start with?

10.† A pupil wishing to find out how much oxygen there is in air connected two syringes by a piece of tubing filled with copper wire. At the start of the experiment there were 100 cm³ of air in the right-hand syringe and the copper was then heated strongly. Every time he passed the air backwards and forwards over the heated copper, the pupil recorded the volume in the right-hand syringe. After six readings he stopped heating, and passed the air over three times more. He obtained the following results:

Volume in right-hand syringe	Number of times the air had been passed backwards and forwards
100 cm³	0
94 cm³	1
90 cm³	2
87 cm³	3
85 cm³	4
83 cm³	5
83 cm³	6 heating stopped here
82 cm³	7
80 cm³	8
80 cm³	9

a. Draw a graph to show how the volume of the gas remaining varied with the number of times the air was passed over the heated copper.
b. At what stage had the reaction ceased?
c. Can you suggest why the volume of the gas decreased slightly after the heating was stopped?
d. What gas remains in the syringe?
e. What value do these figures give for the percentage of oxygen in the air?

11.† When a candle burns in air it loses weight and gradually burns away.
a. Explain why the candle burns away.
b. Name one product formed by the burning of the candle.

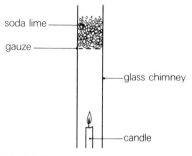

soda lime

gauze

glass chimney

candle

Fig 5.10

c. Why is there only one product formed when either strontium or sulphur burns in air, but more than one product when a candle burns?

12.† When a candle burns, water vapour and a gas X are produced.
a. What is the gas X?
b. What test would you carry out to identify X? Describe what would happen.
c. Which two elements must be present in candle wax?
d. Name one other substance which will burn to give the same pair of products that a candle gives.
e. When a candle is burned under a glass chimney, all the products of combustion can be completely absorbed by some pieces of soda lime, supported on gauze, as shown in Fig 5.10. When the candle burns, will the total mass of the candle, chimney and contents increase, decrease or remain the same?
f. Explain your answer to e.
g. Some wax from a candle is heated carefully until it boils. It is found to start boiling at 320°C, but does not completely boil away until the temperature has reached 400°C. Suggest an explanation for this.

13.
a. What experiments would you do to show that we breathe out more carbon dioxide than we breathe in? (Remember that air contains a little carbon dioxide.)
b. Where does the extra carbon dioxide come from?
c. Which gas is less common in the air that we breathe out than in the air we breathe in?

14. What experiment would you carry out to prove that *nitrogen* and water together do not cause rusting?

15.
a. In what ways are burning, breathing and rusting similar?
b. How does rusting differ from burning and breathing?

16.† Three boys are talking about rusting. Each makes one of the following remarks:
a. All kinds of iron rust.

61

b. Galvanized iron (iron covered with a layer of zinc) doesn't rust.
c. Dry iron doesn't rust.
   Write instructions for experiments to find out which boys are right and which are wrong. You get marks for planning the experiments, not for knowing the correct answers.

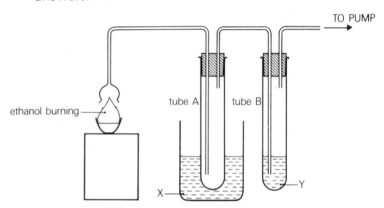

Fig 5.11

17. The apparatus shown in Fig 5.11 can be used to show that carbon dioxide and water are produced when ethanol is burned.
a. Suggest what substance X might be.
b. Water collects in tube A and must have left the flame as a gas. What has happened to it to make it visible in tube A?
c. How would you show that the substance in tube A was water?
d. What would the substance Y be?
e. How would this substance show that carbon dioxide was present?
f. Why must tube A come before tube B?
g. What would you see in tubes A and B if the experiment were repeated, but with the burning ethanol removed so that only air was drawn through the apparatus?

18. An apparatus is set up as in Fig 5.12 and the red lead oxide is heated. The syringes move out. The gas is then passed over the copper which is heated. Eventually the copper turns completely black, but a little gas remains.

a. Why do the syringes move out when the red lead oxide is heated?
b. Why does the copper blacken and the volume get less?
c. Why is a little gas left at the end?
d. Is the gas given off by the red lead oxide the same as the gas that turns the copper black?
e. How would you alter the experiment to try to make sure that *all* the gas had been used up by the end?
f. If all the gas were used up, how would the loss in mass of the red lead oxide compare with the gain in mass of the copper?

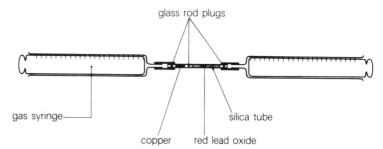

Fig 5.12

Background reading

The discovery of oxygen and the modern idea of burning
Modern ideas of burning were put forward in 1774 by a French chemist called Antoine Lavoisier. Until that time chemists had believed that substances lost something called **phlogiston** when they burned. This **phlogiston theory** could be summarized:

SUBSTANCE $\xrightarrow{\text{burning}}$ CALX + PHLOGISTON
(or ash)

This was presumably based on the observation that many substances (for example magnesium and wood) tend to crumble when they burn and look as though they have lost something.

As chemists began to weigh the substances they heated, the phlogiston theory became more difficult to uphold; how can substances *gain* mass on burning (as they do) while *losing* phlogiston? So sure were many chemists of the

63

validity of the phlogiston theory that they invented ingenious ways around this problem, some even suggesting that phlogiston had negative mass!

Around 1774 several chemists had in fact prepared the gas we now call oxygen by various methods; these men included Scheele, a Swedish chemist, and the Englishman Priestley. Priestley had decomposed mercury oxide by heating it and had obtained a gas in which candles and other materials burned more brightly than in air. He also noticed that a mouse lived longer in the gas and that his 'breast felt peculiarly light and easy for some time afterwards' when he tried breathing it. Priestley called the gas **dephlogisticated air** concluding that substances burned more vigorously because it took up their phlogiston readily. Priestley's main contribution was that he told Lavoisier of his discovery when they met in Paris in October 1774. Lavoisier repeated the experiment but realized it led not to an extension of the phlogiston theory, but to a new theory of burning – the one we hold today.

To verify this, he heated mercury in a furnace using a retort as shown in Fig 5.13. After a while he noticed the 'red calx of mercury' (mercury oxide) forming on the surface of the mercury. After 12 days no further change had occurred and the volume of air in the bell-jar had fallen from 50 cubic inches to 42 cubic inches. Thus the mercury had *taken in* part of the air when it formed its calx. He then took the mercury calx, scraping it away from the mercury, and heated it in a small retort. He collected 8 cubic inches of gas, exactly the volume lost by the air. He also showed that the gas had the same properties as Priestley's dephlogisticated air. When this gas was added back to the 42 cubic inches of gas in the bell-jar, the resulting mixture could not be distinguished from ordinary air. All this led Lavoisier to put forward the theory that mercury *combined* with this newly discovered gas to form its calx.

MERCURY + OXYGEN $\rightleftharpoons$ MERCURY OXIDE

He concluded that the gas Priestley had discovered was the 'active part' of the air. His name 'oxygen' means 'acid former' as he thought that all oxides were acidic (in fact only those of the non-metals are, see Chapter 8).

Fig 5.13 Lavoisier's experiment

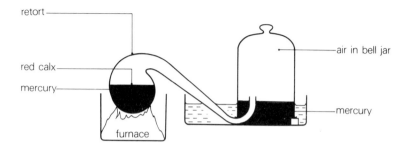

Questions
1. What fraction of the air was used up in Lavoisier's experiment? Can you suggest why this is not the 20% you might expect?
2. Write a letter that Lavoisier might have written to try to convince Priestley that the phlogiston theory was wrong. (You need not write it in French!)
3. Is the reaction studied by Lavoisier a temporary or permanent change?
4. Draw a diagram of a modern laboratory apparatus with which *you* could repeat Lavoisier's experiment. **(Do not attempt this experiment without supervision as mercury vapour is poisonous.)**

Further reading
Partington, *A short history of chemistry*. Macmillan (mainly for teachers)
Anderson, *Burning and Lavoisier*. Revised Nuffield Chemistry study sheets. Longman
Film
History of the Discovery of Oxygen. ICI

Chapter 6 **Chemical reactions**

6.1 Chemical changes

The reactions described in the last two Chapters have all been chemical changes. If a chemical change takes place the **products** of the reaction have very different chemical properties from the **reactants** (the substances which react together). Let us consider a few examples:

1. Sulphur reacts with the oxygen in the air:

SULPHUR	+	OXYGEN	⟶	SULPHUR DIOXIDE
yellow solid		colourless gas		colourless gas
		no smell		sharp smell
melts at 119°C		boils at —183°C		boils at —10°C

An entirely new substance has been produced from the original sulphur and oxygen. They have not mixed but have *reacted* together to form the compound sulphur dioxide.

2. The loss of carbon dioxide from copper carbonate:

COPPER CARBONATE $\xrightarrow{\text{heat}}$ COPPER OXIDE + CARBON DIOXIDE
green solid   black solid   colourless gas

Here the copper carbonate changes chemically (in this case, *decomposes*) into the products which have very different properties from the reactants. (Copper carbonate is obviously not a mixture of copper oxide and carbon dioxide.)

3. The air consists mainly of the two colourless, odourless gases, oxygen and nitrogen. In the air these are *mixed* together and the properties of the air are a mixture of the properties of oxygen and the properties of nitrogen. If air is raised to a very high temperature (as, for example in a lightning flash) a chemical reaction occurs and a

compound is formed:

NITROGEN	+	OXYGEN	$\longrightarrow$	NITROGEN DIOXIDE
colourless gas		colourless gas		brown gas
no smell		no smell		distinct smell

The product is very different from the mixture of nitrogen and oxygen in air. Air can be separated into nitrogen and oxygen by fractional distillation (see Section 2.5) but a chemical reaction is needed to break down the compound nitrogen dioxide.

4. As a final example, consider a mixture of iron and sulphur, part metal and part yellow solid. The iron can be separated by using a magnet, or the sulphur can be dissolved in a solvent such as hot toluene. However, when the mixture is heated a reaction occurs and a *compound*, iron sulphide is formed:

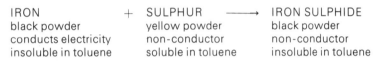

IRON	+	SULPHUR	$\longrightarrow$	IRON SULPHIDE
black powder		yellow powder		black powder
conducts electricity		non-conductor		non-conductor
insoluble in toluene		soluble in toluene		insoluble in toluene

The iron cannot be removed from the iron sulphide by a magnet and no part of it is soluble in toluene. Once again the product is very different from the reactants and cannot be separated except by a chemical reaction.

Summary

A *mixture* of substances has the properties of these substances and can usually be separated by physical methods (for example, sieving, filtering, dissolving, distilling, etc.) whereas a *compound* has its own properties and can only be broken down by a chemical reaction. A chemical reaction results in different substances with different properties being formed.

6.2 Evidence for chemical reaction

It is often easy to tell that a reaction has occurred by

observing that the *properties* have changed. For example, from Section 6.1 evidence that a reaction had occurred would be:

1. Sulphur dioxide has a smell which is different from that of sulphur or oxygen.
2. Copper carbonate, which is green, gives a black solid when it has been heated.
3. Nitrogen and oxygen (colourless gases) react to form nitrogen dioxide (a brown gas).
4. Iron and sulphur (black and yellow specks) react to form iron sulphide (all black).

Other examples we have met earlier are:

5. Dry blue copper sulphate crystals give a white powder and water when heated.
6. Magnesium (a shiny metal) and oxygen (gas) react to form magnesium oxide (white powder).

As many chemical reactions give out energy when they occur, it is also possible to detect a reaction in this way. For example, grey zinc powder reacts with yellow sulphur to produce zinc sulphide which is white. The energy is given out as light and intense heat, and a cloud of white smoke (zinc sulphide) rises from the reaction. **(Warning – this reaction can be dangerous.)**

Heat is the commonest way in which energy is released during chemical reactions. Anhydrous copper sulphate reacting with water becomes warm and magnesium reacting with oxygen gets very hot. All burning reactions give off heat which is one reason why they are so useful to us.

Light is also given out during reactions; magnesium reacting with oxygen gives white light, sulphur burning in oxygen gives a blue flame and candlelight was used as a source of illumination for many years. Another form of energy which is sometimes observed is sound; for example, the 'pop' when hydrogen reacts with oxygen or the bang resulting from a chemical explosion.

It is therefore possible to use eyes, ears and nose to detect a reaction. However the most valuable 'sense' in these cases is that of touch. It becomes second nature for a chemist to touch a test-tube to try to detect the temperature rise which tells him that a chemical reaction has almost certainly taken place.

6.3 The masses of substances which react

When zinc is *mixed* with sulphur any amount of zinc can be mixed with any amount of sulphur. 1 gram of zinc could be mixed with 10 grams of sulphur, or 5 grams of zinc could be mixed with 1 gram of sulphur, and so on. However when zinc *reacts* with sulphur it can only do so in one ratio. It is found that 1 gram of zinc always reacts with just less than $\frac{1}{2}$ gram of sulphur; the masses of the elements will always be present in the same *proportion* in the zinc sulphide which is formed. A compound always contains its elements combined in a definite proportion.

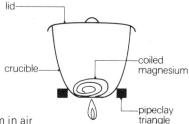

Fig 6.1 Burning magnesium in air

When magnesium reacts with oxygen the masses of each substance which combine are in proportion. Magnesium can be burned in a crucible (Fig 6.1). The lid must be lifted from time to time to let in more oxygen, but the experimenter must take care to avoid losing magnesium oxide as a white smoke. The magnesium and the crucible (plus lid) are weighed separately before the experiment, and the crucible, lid and magnesium oxide are weighed at the end. The mass of magnesium oxide can be worked out by subtracting the mass of crucible and lid from the second weighing. Several of these experiments can be done and the results presented as a graph by plotting *mass of magnesium* on the horizontal axis against *mass of magnesium oxide* (Fig 6.2). The graph should be a straight line which passes through the origin. This shows that the masses of magnesium and the corresponding masses of magnesium oxide are always in the same proportion. If a graph is plotted of mass of reactant

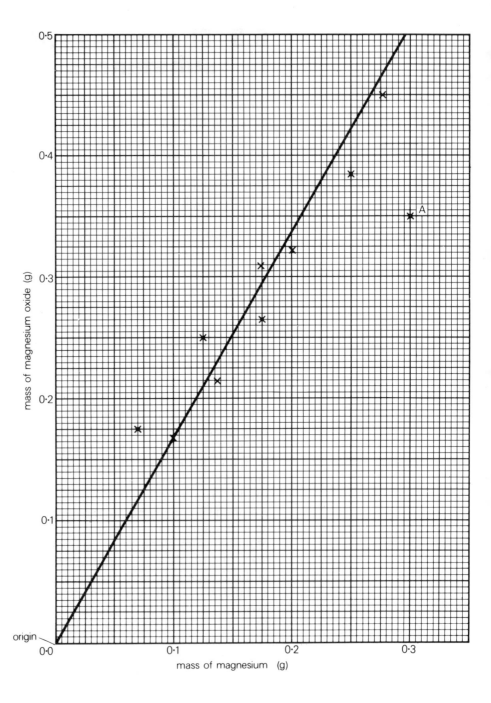

Fig 6.2

against corresponding mass of product in a chemical reaction, a straight line will always be obtained.

Summary

1. The differences between mixtures and compounds may be summarized.

Mixtures	Compounds
may be separated by physical methods	separated by chemical reactions only
have properties of the substances which are mixed together	have their own properties
substances can be mixed in any proportion	substances react to form compounds in a definite proportion

2. Chemical reactions can be recognized from the following signs:
a. New substance formed.
b. Heat or light given out.

Questions

1. When brown copper reacts with yellow sulphur, a glow spreads through the test-tube and a black solid is left.
a. Why is there a glow?
b. Is the black solid a compound (copper sulphide) or a mixture of copper and sulphur? Give reasons for your answer.
c. Why are the amounts of copper and sulphur important in this experiment?

2. When a match is struck, it burns.
a. How many senses could tell you that a chemical reaction is taking place?
b. What would each sense tell you?

3. Are the following examples of chemical reactions or physical changes? Give reasons for each of your answers.
a. A gas fire burning.
b. An electric fire getting hot.
c. Cobalt chloride turning from blue to pink when heated.
d. Ice turning to water when heated.
e. Salt dissolving in water.
f. Carbon (charcoal) burning in oxygen.
g. A copper roof slowly turning green over the years.

4.† A bright red powder (a metal oxide) is heated; a colourless gas is produced and a yellow residue remains.
a. What evidence do you have that a chemical reaction is taking place?
b. What do you think the colourless gas is?
c. How would you test for this gas? What would you expect the result to be?

5.†
a. Give two reasons for believing that the addition of water to anhydrous copper sulphate results in a chemical reaction.
b. Give two reasons for believing that magnesium oxide is a compound and not a mixture of magnesium and oxygen.

6. Say, giving your reasons, whether you think the following are mixtures or compounds.
   a. Milk   d. Copper oxide.
   b. Ice.   e. Carbon dioxide.
   c. Orange juice   f. Paint.

7. 5 grams of calcium combine with 2 grams of oxygen to form 7 grams of calcium oxide. Assuming that this is the only compound formed between calcium and oxygen, how much calcium oxide would you expect to get from:
a. 10 grams calcium and 4 grams oxygen?
b. 10 grams calcium and 2 grams oxygen?
c. 5 grams calcium and 4 grams oxygen?

8. Refer to the graph in Fig 6.2.
a. Explain in your own words why the graph is a straight line.

b. Why has the point A been ignored when the line was drawn?
c. What mistake may have been made by the group who obtained point A?
d. Using your graph, work out the mass of oxygen which combines with 0.1 g magnesium.
e. How much oxygen would combine with 1 g of magnesium?
f. A class of pupils repeat the experiment but they use magnesium from an old sample which is already partly oxidized on the surface. They plot their results, *mass of magnesium taken* against *mass of magnesium oxide* and they obtain a straight-line graph. Say, giving your reasons, where this line will be in relation to the line in Fig 6.2.

Chapter 7 **Acids and alkalis**

7.1 The pH scale

As you go through a chemistry course, you will find that the meaning of the word '**acid**' changes gradually. To start with we say that an acid is a substance which is sour to the taste, though tasting is to be avoided since many acids are poisonous! The word acid often suggests a substance which burns or corrodes, but many acids are quite harmless. Indeed much of what we eat and drink is acid and it would taste very dull if it were not. The 'opposite' of an acid is an **alkali**. Alkalis are often much more harmful than acids and they should be treated with great care. A substance which is

Table 7.1 The pH values of some common substances

Laboratory	pH value		Home
hydrochloric, nitric and sulphuric acids	0	STRONG ACID	car battery acid
	1		
iron (III) chloride	2		lemon juice
acetic acid	3		beer, sour milk
	4	WEAK ACID	eating apple
ammonium chloride, carbon dioxide	5		
	6		fresh milk
	7	NEUTRAL	salt, sugar
sodium hydrogencarbonate (bicarbonate)	8		soap, baking powder
sodium acetate	9	WEAK ALKALI	'Milk of magnesia'
	10		
ammonia	11		
limewater (calcium hydroxide) , sodium carbonate	12		washing soda
	13	STRONG ALKALI	oven cleaner
sodium hydroxide, potassium hydroxide	14		

neither acid nor alkali is described as **neutral**. The best example of a neutral substance is pure water.

The acidity and alkalinity of substances can be measured using the pH scale (note – small p, capital H). Neutral substances have a pH of 7, acids have values less than 7 and alkalis have values greater than 7. A very low pH means a very strong acid, whereas a value between 3 and 6 shows a weak acid. The lower the value, the stronger the acid. The opposite applies to alkalis where very high values indicate strongly alkaline solutions. Note that the word *alkaline* is an *adjective* (describing word) and the word *alkali* is a *noun*. Thus we say 'an alkaline solution' but we speak of 'an alkali' not 'an alkaline'.

pH values exist only when the substance is dissolved in water. Thus a completely insoluble substance will not have a pH value. Indicators are used to measure pH values and these are described in Section 7.2.

Table 7.1 shows the pH values of some laboratory substances and also of some found in the home.

7.2 Indicators

It has been known for thousands of years that certain dyes change colour when an acid or an alkali is added to them. These dyes are therefore able to **indicate** the presence of an acid or an alkali. The word **indicator** often implies an acid–alkali indicator, but a substance such as cobalt chloride is also an indicator since it indicates the presence of water.

One of the first indicators was a substance called **litmus**, which was extracted from a species of lichen. In solutions where the pH is 5 or less, litmus turns red; in solutions of pH 8 or more, litmus turns blue, and between 5 and 8 it is a mixture of the two colours. Other indicators change colour at different pH values, as shown in Table 7.2 which gives only a few of the hundreds of possible acid–alkali indicators.

By selecting six or seven indicators which change colour at different pH values, it is possible to make up a **universal indicator**. Such an indicator changes colour gradually over the whole pH range. Often the indicators are chosen so that the colours of the spectrum are obtained, starting with red at

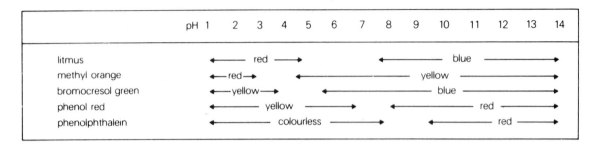

pH	1	2	3	4	5	6	7	8	9	10	11	12	13	14
litmus		← red →						←		blue				→
methyl orange	← red →		←				yellow							→
bromocresol green	← yellow →		←				blue							→
phenol red	←		yellow			→	←		red				→	
phenolphthalein	←		colourless			→	←		red				→	

Table 7.2 The colours of some indicators. In the 'gaps' shown the indicators are changing from one colour to the other

the acid end (red, orange, yellow, green, blue, indigo, violet). There are several universal indicators and they are not all quite the same, for example the neutral colour is orange-yellow, yellow or green in three different universal indicators. The colours of indicators at various pH values are often shown on the bottles. The indicators are supplied in two forms. One is a solution in ethanol (alcohol) and the other is paper which has been soaked in the indicator solution and dried. This is often known as **pH paper**.

The simplest way to find an unknown pH is to use universal indicator. The substance with the unknown pH is dissolved in water, the indicator paper is added and half a minute is allowed for it to develop the true colour. If a solution of universal indicator is used then one drop should be added to the unknown solution. If the pH of a gas is required it may be tested with damp indicator paper.

7.3 Neutralization

If an alkali is added to an acid, the alkali reacts with the acid and some of the acidity is **neutralized**. If more alkali is added, more of the acid is neutralized until enough alkali has been added to make the solution exactly neutral. This is a difficult point to obtain and often too much alkali is added and the pH goes right through from a low value to a high one. However, with care it is possible to add just enough alkali to neutralize the acid.

Acids are substances which contain hydrogen, though their names do not always show this. An alternative name for hydrochloric acid is hydrogen chloride; sulphuric acid could be called hydrogen sulphate, and nitric acid hydrogen nitrate. The names of alkalis usually end in 'hydroxide'. When an acid reacts with an alkali the hydrogen reacts with the hydroxide to give hydrogen hydroxide, which is usually called water. For example:

SODIUM HYDROXIDE $+$ HYDROGEN CHLORIDE $\longrightarrow$ HYDROGEN HYDROXIDE (water) $+$ SODIUM CHLORIDE (common salt)

Both the substances produced are neutral.
Another example is:

POTASSIUM HYDROXIDE $+$ HYDROGEN SULPHATE (sulphuric acid) $\longrightarrow$ HYDROGEN HYDROXIDE (water) $+$ POTASSIUM SULPHATE

The chlorides, sulphates and nitrates of metals are members of the large group of substances which chemists call **salts**. Sodium chloride, which is called salt in everyday language is only one of many salts in chemical language, so it is called **common salt** to distinguish it. You will find more about salts in Chapter 11.

The general equation for neutralization is:

ACID $+$ ALKALI $\longrightarrow$ SALT $+$ WATER

Neutralization is certainly a chemical reaction since entirely new products are formed. Also heat is given out; such reactions are said to be **exothermic**.

The equation is sometimes expressed:

ACID $+$ BASE $\longrightarrow$ SALT $+$ WATER

A **base** is any substance which will react with an acid to form a salt. As we shall see in the next Chapter (Section 8.4) metals form oxides which are bases. Most metals form oxides which, though they are insoluble in water, dissolve in acids just enough to neutralize them. Some metals form oxides which are soluble in water (and can still neutralize acids) and these are called **alkalis** (*soluble* bases). For example, sodium oxide is an alkali and it dissolves in water to form sodium hydroxide solution.

7.4 Applications of neutralization

People are often tempted to deal with the spillage of acids and alkalis using neutralization. If the spillage is on skin or clothing the neutralizing acid or alkali can be more dangerous than the substance which is spilt. The treatment here is washing and drenching with water, since acids and alkalis are soluble in water. If the spillage is on the bench or floor, then neutralization is used. If a concentrated acid is spilt, the neutralizing agent is a *weak* alkali. Normally sodium carbonate or sodium hydrogencarbonate solution are used. These fizz (Chapter 11) if acid is still present. The reason for using a weak alkali is that it is easy to add too much. An excess of weak alkali is fairly harmless but an excess of strong alkali would be just as dangerous as the original spilled acid. For similar reasons a strong alkali is normally neutralized with dilute acetic acid. If more than enough is added a vinegary smell persists.

The stomach contains acid to help in the process of digestion. Sometimes too much acid is present and this is the commonest cause of indigestion ('acid stomach'). Some of the acid can be neutralized by a suitable very mild alkali. Milk of Magnesia (a suspension of magnesium hydroxide in water) is one of the remedies which is used and such medicines are sometimes called **antacids**. If the indigestion persists, a doctor should be consulted.

Neutralization is important in agriculture. The pH of soil can be measured by first shaking it with water and barium sulphate. The very insoluble barium sulphate helps the soil particles to settle at the bottom of the tube and the solution which remains can then be tested with indicator in the usual way. Plants will grow only in soils where the pH value lies between 6 and 8. Many plants like a neutral pH, but some grow better if the pH is a little lower than 7, while others prefer a slightly alkaline pH.

The more common problem is a soil which is too acid. In this case lime (calcium hydroxide) (Section 11.7) is added to neutralize the acid and increase the pH. Where soils are alkaline, acid fertilizers (ammonium nitrate or ammonium sulphate, which are added to replace nitrogen compounds lost by the soil) will lower the pH.

Summary

1. Acids are substances which have a sour taste and a pH less than 7.* Alkalis have a pH greater than 7.
2. Substances which change colour in the presence of acids or alkalis are called *indicators*. A universal indicator shows different colours at different pH values.
3. The reaction between acids and alkalis is called **neutralization** and the general equation is:

ACID + ALKALI ⟶ SALT + WATER

Questions

1.
a. Explain how you would try to measure the pH of a colourless solution.
b. What values would you expect if the solution was:
  i Citric acid?
  ii Sodium chloride?
  iii Lime (calcium hydroxide)?

2.† Four test-tubes contain dilute solutions of vinegar, washing soda, salt and sulphuric acid. You are not sure which contains which, so you add a few drops of universal indicator to each tube. From the following results, write down which substance is in each of the four tubes.

Tube	Colour	pH
1	red	2
2	orange	4
3	green	7
4	blue	10

* A further definition of an acid is a substance containing hydrogen which can be displaced by a reactive metal (see Section 10.1).

3.[†] There is an indicator which gives a yellow colour when added to lemon juice, a blue colour when added to Milk of Magnesia, and is green when added to pure water. Some of the indicator was added to a solution of slaked lime, and then hydrochloric acid was run in slowly, with shaking, until there was no further change of colour. Write down the three colours – yellow, blue and green – in the *order* in which they would be seen.

4.
a. What is meant by neutralization?
b. Why is neutralization important to a farmer?
c. How can neutralization be used to cure indigestion?

5. If a strong concentrated acid is spilt on the floor, a weak alkali, sodium hydrogencarbonate, is used to neutralize it.
a. How do we know when the acid has been completely neutralized by the sodium hydrogencarbonate?
b. Why isn't a strong alkali used instead?
c. Why isn't water used in *this* case?

6.
a. What is the first aid treatment if some strong concentrated acid is accidentally spilt on your hand?
b. Why isn't the acid neutralized with an alkali?

7. An old wives mnemonic (memory aid) for treating bee and wasp stings is '*Bee–Bicarb; Vinegar-Vasp*'. *Bicarb* is sodium hydrogen carbonate, a weak alkali; vinegar is a weak acid. What does the treatment suggest to you about the nature of bee and wasp stings?

8.[†] Two companies advertise pills which they say relieve stomach ache by neutralizing the acid in the stomach. Describe experiments that you would do:
a. To check that the pills do in fact neutralize acids.
b. To discover which one neutralizes the most acid.

9.[†] You are provided with universal indicator paper and a supply of 'gripe water', which can be used as a medicine to cure stomach acidity.
a. What would you expect to observe if the indicator paper is wetted with the gripe water?

b. Describe how you could use the gripe water and indicator paper in an experiment to discover whether bottles of 'malt vinegar' or 'wine vinegar', bought from the grocer, contain different concentrations of acid.

10.† An acid solution and alkaline solution were mixed in the volumes given below and the resulting solutions were tested with indicator. One mixture was neutral (pH 7), one had a pH value of 13 and the third had a pH value of 1.

Copy out the table and fill in the column headed pH value.

Volume of acid (cm³)	Volume of alkali (cm³)	pH value
20	13	
20	15	
20	17	

11.†
a. Suggest how you could measure the pH of a dry sample of soil in the laboratory.
b. What pH value would you expect acidic soil to have?
c. Which one of the following substances would be most suitable for neutralizing this acidic soil?
Salt, water, lime, sand, vinegar.
d. What would happen to the pH of the soil when you added this substance?

12.† There is a type of vegetable which is normally green in colour, but which turns red if cooked with vinegar.
a. Describe the method by which you would try to extract and separate the coloured substances in the green vegetable leaves.
b. How would you try to find out which of these coloured substances changes colour when treated with vinegar?
c. What is the name given to the type of substance which changes colour in this way?
d. Describe experiments which you could do to discover whether it is the cooking or the vinegar that turns the colour from green to red.

13. What products would you expect when the following react together?
a. Sodium hydroxide and nitric acid (hydrogen nitrate).
b. Potassium hydroxide and hydrochloric acid (hydrogen chloride).
c. Ammonium hydroxide and sulphuric acid (hydrogen sulphate).
d. In each case the salt is obtained as a solution in water. How would you obtain crystals of the salts?

14.
a. Use the information in Table 7.2 and the information below to deduce what you can about the pH values of:
  i Carbon dioxide solution.
  ii Ammonia solution.
  iii Sulphur dioxide solution.

Solution	Methyl orange colour	Litmus colour	Phenolphthalein colour
carbon dioxide	yellow	red	colourless
ammonia	yellow	blue	red
sulphur dioxide	red	red	colourless

b. Do you think that a mixture of methyl orange, litmus and phenolphthalein would make a good universal indicator? Give your reasons.

Background reading

The names of acids and alkalis
The word 'alkali' comes from the Arabic and means 'the ashes', since the ashes from burning plant and animal materials are alkaline. 'Kalium', the name most other languages use for potassium, is derived from alkali. The name 'potassium' comes from *potash* (potassium carbonate) which gets its name from the way it used to be made. Wood ashes were dissolved in water and the solution evaporated in pots. The old name for potassium hydroxide was **caustic potash**; 'caustic' means 'burning', and brings home the dangerous nature of potassium hydroxide.

Sodium carbonate is called **soda** or **washing soda** to distinguish it from sodium hydroxide which is **caustic soda**.

Lime is the name given to alkaline substances containing calcium. Calcium oxide is known as **quicklime** or **caustic lime**; calcium hydroxide is known as **slaked lime**, **milk of lime**, and, in solution, as **limewater**. Calcium carbonate, which is much less soluble in water than sodium or potassium carbonates, is known as **limestone**. These compounds are considered again in Chapter 11.

Acids generally have much more obvious names. Sulphuric acid contains sulphur, though concentrated sulphuric acid used to be known as **oil of vitriol** and the adjective 'vitriolic' is still used today.

Chapter 8 **The chemical elements**

8.1 **Elements and compounds**

We first met the term *element* in Chapter 5 when we were looking at substances which burned in air. You will remember that an element, when it burns, gives a single oxide. This ties in with the definition of an element as a substance which cannot be broken down into anything simpler by chemical means. Some naturally occurring substances, such as nitrogen, oxygen and gold, are elements. Other elements, such as copper, can be extracted from their compounds fairly easily; while metals such as sodium and potassium can be obtained only with difficulty. In all there are 90 naturally occurring elements. Since 1940 man has managed to make another 15, all of which are dangerously radioactive. Of the ninety, less than forty are common enough to be met outside universities.

Any single substance which is not an element is a *compound*. A compound can be defined as a substance consisting of two or more elements chemically combined together. In Chapter 5 we found that when compounds burn they usually give a mixture of the oxides of the elements which they contain. In Chapter 6 we learned more about compounds and saw how they differed from mixtures of elements. Thus *definite amounts* of the elements zinc and sulphur combine together in a *chemical reaction* to form the *compound* zinc sulphide. A mixture of zinc and sulphur remains a mixture of elements rather than a compound.

The names of compounds often show which elements they contain. For example, copper sulph*ide* contains copper and sulphur, chemically combined together. The ending

-*ide* means that only sulphur is present with copper, but the ending -*ate* means that oxygen is also present. Thus copper sulph*ate* contains copper, sulphur *and oxygen* chemically combined together.

8.2 Metals and non-metals

Obviously life would be difficult for chemists if they had to remember the details of 100 elements and their compounds. Fortunately several elements often resemble each other and behave in the same way, so it is possible to classify the elements into large sets, and then divide them into sub-sets. Thus it is possible to forecast how an element will behave if we know which set it is in. The first division involves classifying the elements into two sets, the metals and the non-metals.

8.3 Physical properties of the elements

Metallic elements can often be recognized because they shine brightly at a freshly cut or scraped surface. They can also be hammered into different shapes without breaking and are said to be **malleable**. Blacksmiths, silversmiths and goldsmiths all make use of this property of malleability of the metals with which they work. Non-metals by contrast are **brittle**.

Another way of recognizing a metal is that it will conduct electricity very well. This can be seen by using the apparatus in Fig 8.1. Not only do metals conduct electricity well but they are also good conductors of heat, as you will know if you have ever tried to touch the handle of a poker which has been left in a fire. (See *Physics 11–13*, page 253.)

Most non-metals are poor conductors of heat and electricity, but there is one exception. One of the forms of the element carbon, called graphite, is a fairly good conductor

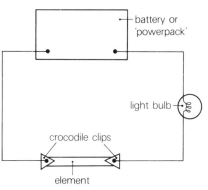

battery or 'powerpack'

light bulb

crocodile clips

element

Fig 8.1 Testing the conductivity of an element

Element	Type	Melting point (°C)	Density (g per cm³)	Nature of oxide	Solubility of oxide	pH of oxide solution
carbon	non-metal	very high	2.2	gas	fairly soluble	4.5
hydrogen	non-metal	−259	0.00008	liquid	soluble	7
phosphorus	non-metal	44	1.8	solid – low melting point	very soluble – violent reaction	0
sulphur	non-metal	113	2.1	gas	soluble	1
copper	everyday metal	1080	8.9	black solid	insoluble	
iron	everyday metal	1540	7.9	black or brown solid	insoluble	
lead	everyday metal	327	11.4	yellow, red or brown solid	insoluble	
zinc	everyday metal	419	7.1	white solid (yellow when hot)	insoluble	
calcium	reactive metal	850	1.6	white solid	fairly soluble	12
magnesium	reactive metal	650	1.7	white solid	sparingly soluble	9
potassium	reactive metal	64	0.9	white solid	very soluble	14
sodium	reactive metal	98	1.0	white solid	very soluble	14

Table 8.1 The properties of some elements

of electricity, though the other form of carbon (diamond) is a bad conductor like all the other non-metallic elements.

Measurement of melting point is not a good way of distinguishing metals from non-metals. Most metals have a higher melting point than most non-metals, but there are exceptions. Carbon and some other non-metals have very high melting points, while metals such as sodium melt at low temperatures (see Table 8.1). However, it is possible to say that if an element is a gas at room temperature it must be a non-metal. There are only two elements which are liquids at room temperature – bromine (a non-metal) and mercury (a metal).

The densities of metals vary widely and it is helpful here to divide the set of metals into two sub-sets: 'reactive metals' and 'everyday metals'. We meet 'reactive metals' (sodium, calcium, etc.) as elements only in the laboratory, since they are too reactive to be used to make common articles. However, we are familiar with objects made from copper, iron, etc., so these are termed 'everyday metals'. It is found that 'everyday metals' have a higher density than non-metals but 'reactive metals' are less dense than many non-metals (see Table 8.1).

8.4 The oxides of elements

We saw in Chapter 5 that many substances react with oxygen, and that the behaviour of their oxides provides another way of distinguishing between metals and non-metals. The first difference is that the oxides of non-metals usually have low melting and boiling points, so they are either gases, liquids or volatile solids at room temperature. Metal oxides all have high melting and boiling points.

The other way of distinguishing between metal and non-metal oxides is by finding out whether they are acids or bases (see Chapter 7). Non-metal oxides dissolve in water to give a pH which is less than 7, that is they are acidic. Metal oxides are bases – they neutralize acids to form salts. For example, if copper oxide is stirred with hot sulphuric acid and the excess solid is filtered off, the filtrate is blue as it contains copper sulphate.

COPPER OXIDE + HYDROGEN SULPHATE ⟶ COPPER SULPHATE + HYDROGEN OXIDE
                (sulphuric acid)   (water)

Copper oxide is insoluble in water and so, although it is a base, it is not an alkali. In general the metals that we meet in everyday life are those which form insoluble basic oxides and these oxides are often coloured. It is the reactive metals which form oxides which produce alkaline solutions, as Table 8.1 shows. Thus we can say that:

most non-metals form oxides which have low melting points and are acidic;

most metals form oxides which have high melting points and are basic, some also being alkaline.

This is illustrated by the Venn diagram (Fig 8.2).

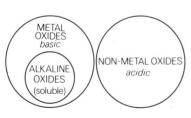

Fig 8.2 The oxides of the elements

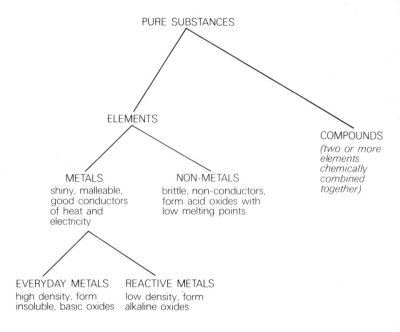

Fig 8.3 A summary of Chapter 8

PURE SUBSTANCES

ELEMENTS

COMPOUNDS
(two or more elements chemically combined together)

METALS
shiny, malleable, good conductors of heat and electricity

NON-METALS
brittle, non-conductors, form acid oxides with low melting points

EVERYDAY METALS
high density, form insoluble, basic oxides

REACTIVE METALS
low density, form alkaline oxides

Summary

We have seen that pure substances can first be divided into elements and compounds. Elements can be divided into metals and non-metals, and metals can be divided into 'everyday' and 'reactive' metals. This can be summed up in a diagram (Fig 8.3).

Further classification of the chemical elements can be made; this leads to the Periodic table, a topic which is beyond the scope of this book.

Questions

1.
a. What is meant by a chemical element?
b. What is a chemical compound?
c. How does a mixture of hydrogen and oxygen differ from the compound water (hydrogen oxide)?

2.[†] Single pure chemical substances may be either elements or compounds, and elements may be either metals or non-metals. Divide the following six substances into:
a. Metallic elements.

b. Non-metallic elements.
c. Compounds.
Calcium, carbon, copper sulphate, mercury, nitrogen, water.

3.[†] Everyday substances around us are either elements, compounds or mixtures. Give one example of each of these and state in each case why you believe it to belong to that group.

4.[†] Choose from the following list of substances:
a. An element.
b. A solid compound.
c. A mixture.
d. An acidic oxide.
e. A solid conductor of electricity.
f. A neutral oxide.
Carbon dioxide, copper, acetone (propanone), copper sulphate, sea water, magnesium oxide, oxygen, pure water, sulphur, air.

5.[†]
a. i What have copper, iron, sulphur and tin in common?
   ii How does sulphur differ from the other members of the group?
b. i What have carbon dioxide, iron oxide, sulphur dioxide and water in common?
   ii In what way does iron oxide differ from the other members of the group?

6.[†] A boy found a lump of a yellow mineral which he thought was either sulphur or gold.
a. What can he deduce from the following experimental results?
It did not conduct electricity.
It did not melt when heated with a Bunsen burner.
It did not catch fire when heated in air.
b. Could the mineral be either sulphur or gold?

7.[†] Describe two differences (other than colour) which you would expect to find between a cylinder of copper metal and a roll of sulphur which are exactly the same size and shape.

8. Classify the following elements as reactive metals, everyday metals or non-metals. Give your reasons.

a. A gas, A, which burns to give a liquid oxide, pH 7.

b. A gas, B, which forms no oxide.

c. A liquid, C, which conducts electricity well and forms a red insoluble oxide.

d. A solid, D, which is very shiny and which forms a black insoluble oxide.

e. A solid, E, which reacts rapidly in air to form a whitish oxide that is very soluble (pH 14).

f. A black solid, F, which is a good conductor of electricity and burns to give a soluble gaseous oxide (pH 4.5).

g. A solid, G, which is a poor conductor of electricity and which forms a very soluble white acidic oxide.

h. A shiny solid, H, which is a good conductor but is chemically not very reactive.

If you can, deduce the names of the elements A, C and F.

9.† Study carefully the properties of the substances recorded in the table below.

Substance	Electrical conductivity	What happens when heated in air
A	good	becomes coated with film of oxide
B	none	burns to give carbon dioxide and water
C	good	burns very vigorously
D	none	melts and burns with a blue flame
E	fair	glows red hot and produces a gas that turns limewater milky

a. Which of the substances A–E is a compound? Give a reason for your answer.

b. Which two of the substances are metallic elements? Which is the more reactive?

c. Suggest a name for one of these two metallic elements, giving the letter of the substance you are naming.

d. Suggest what the element D might be.

e. What is substance E?

10. State, giving your reasons, whether you think that the lettered substances are elements, compounds or mixtures.

a. W burned readily to give water and a gas that turned limewater milky.

b. X melted over a wide range of temperature: on further heating, its boiling point gradually rose as it was distilled.

c. Y melted sharply at 337°C and then gave off a gas which rekindled a glowing splint.

d. Z melted sharply and then burned to give only one oxide.

11.[†] The table below gives information about six actual elements which are disguised by the letters A–F.

State which letter in the table refers to:

a. Copper.   c. Oxygen.
b. Mercury.   d. Sodium.

Give your reasons in each case.

Element	Melting point (°C)	Does it conduct electricity?	Does it catch fire when heated in air?
A	−259	no	yes
B	−39	yes	no
C	98	yes	yes
D	−219	no	no
E	1083	yes	no
F	119	no	yes

12.[†] In each of the following cases, name an *element* which, when heated in air:

a. Burns with a brilliant flame and leaves a white ash.

b. Melts easily and burns with a blue flame, producing a choking gas.

c. Glows red and produces a gas which turns limewater milky.

13.† Here is a list of some chemical elements:

Argon, calcium, carbon, chlorine, copper, hydrogen, iron, nitrogen, oxygen, sodium, sulphur, zinc.

The question is about pairs of these elements.

a. Which two combine to make water?

b. Which two are the commonest gases in the atmosphere?

c. Which two are solid non-metals?

d. Which two are metals whose oxides form alkaline solutions?

e. Name two from the list which combine to make a sharp-smelling, choking gas.

f. Name two metals from the list which might be found in and around your home.

Background reading

The discovery and naming of the elements

The Ancient Greeks thought that all matter was composed of four elements – earth, air, fire and water. The medieval alchemists held similar views and it was not until the eighteenth century that the elements we know today were recognized as such. Even so, a number of metallic elements were known in classical times, although they were not thought to be elements. Some of them were also associated with particular planets (Table 8.2).

Chemical symbols reflect chemical names and are usually of two letters, though sometimes only one letter is used. The

English name	Symbol	Classical name	Planet
gold	Au	Aurum	(Sun)
silver	Ag	Argentum	(Moon)
mercury	Hg	Hydrargyrum	Mercury
copper	Cu	Cuprum	Venus
iron	Fe	Ferrum	Mars
tin	Sn	Stannum	Jupiter
lead	Pb	Plumbum	Saturn
antimony	Sb	Stibium	

Table 8.2 Some elements known in classical times

first letter is always large and the second letter always small. In Table 8.2 the symbols follow the classical rather than the English names.

Most of the other symbols follow naturally from the English names, but there are some exceptions. The symbol for potassium is K and comes from the Arabic name, 'kalium'. Potassium is still known as kalium in many other languages, just as sodium is known as 'Natrium', which accounts for its symbol, Na. The other exception is the element tungsten whose symbol, W, derives from its other name, 'wolfram'.

In addition to the classical elements, other elements are named after planets, for example uranium (U), plutonium (Pu) and neptunium (Np). These all end -*ium*, an ending common to the more recently discovered metals. Not all elements are named after planets; some are named after places on earth which can vary from small villages, where the element was first found, to vast continents (Table 8.3).

Table 8.3 Some elements which are named after places

Element	Symbol	Origin
strontium	Sr	Strontian, a Scottish village
holmium	Ho	Stockholm, a city
germanium	Ge	Germany, a country
europium	Eu	Europe, a continent

Others are named after people (for example Cm, 'curium' after Marie Curie) or after colours (Cl, chlorine from the Greek word for green). The use of Greek is very common in naming the elements and other examples include hydrogen, H (water former); neon, Ne (new) and bromine, Br (stench).

After classical times, few elements were discovered until the last third of the eighteenth century when a number of non-metals and everday metals were first made. The discovery of electrolysis (Chapter 12) enabled Humphry Davy to make the reactive metals for the first time in 1807 and 1808. Throughout the nineteenth century new elements continued to be discovered and the last non-radioactive element, rhenium, was not discovered until

1925. One of the oddest discoveries was that of the gas helium, which was first discovered on the sun in 1868 (the Greek for sun is helios). It was not until 1895 that it was first isolated on earth by the British scientists Ramsey and Travers, who were preparing all the noble gases for the first time.

Since the application of 'nuclear techniques' in 1940, fifteen new radioactive elements have been made by man, and it is not at all certain how many more new elements will be produced in future. It is unlikely to be a great number, for many of these new elements decompose very rapidly into lighter elements as soon as they are made.

Table 8.4 The number of elements known at various dates

Year	200	1700	1750	1800	1850	1900	1950	2000
Number of elements known	about 10	14	16	33	59	84	97	?

Questions
1. Use a dictionary to try to find out the origins of the following names:
a. Carbon.
b. Chromium.
c. Lithium.
d. Rubidium.
2. After which places are the following named?
   a. Am b. Cf c. Po d. Sc e. Ga and Fr
3. Carbon – C, oxygen – O, potassium – P, sodium – S, uranium – U.
a. Which of the symbols are incorrect?
b. For each element with an incorrect symbol, supply the correct symbol.
c. For each symbol with an incorrect element, supply the correct element.

Chapter 9 # Competition and the affinity series

9.1 Reactivity

In Chapter 8 we saw that it was convenient to divide metals into two classes – 'reactive' and 'everyday' metals. The reason that we meet everyday metals in our daily lives is that they are not very reactive and so do not react quickly with the water vapour or oxygen in the air. But within these two sets there is considerable variation. Gold will not tarnish in air while iron (in the same set) rusts slowly but surely. Therefore we could arrange all the metals in a 'reactivity series' with the 'reactive' metals, such as sodium, at the top, iron somewhere in the middle and gold near the bottom.

There is, however, a snag which we have to overcome when getting information to place the metals in the series. Iron can exist as a fine powder (iron filings) and as large chunks (for example, iron nails). The filings burn like a sparkler firework, but the nail merely glows when heated. So reactivity depends not only on the nature of the metal, but also on its physical state (whether it is in very small or large pieces). A better way of arranging the metals in order is to let them compete with one another for a non-metallic element, usually oxygen.

9.2 Affinity for oxygen

If magnesium powder and copper oxide are mixed together on an unreactive metal dish and the dish is then heated, a violent reaction occurs. This is much more violent than when magnesium powder on its own is heated in the same way. We therefore suspect that a reaction has taken place and we can represent the reaction by a 'word equation':

MAGNESIUM + COPPER OXIDE ⟶ MAGNESIUM OXIDE + COPPER

95

The magnesium has 'grabbed' the oxygen from the copper oxide and we say that the magnesium has a greater **affinity** for the oxygen than copper.

If iron filings are mixed with magnesium oxide and the mixture is heated, no reaction occurs between them. The black specks of iron and white specks of magnesium oxide can still be seen at the end. But if iron filings are heated with copper oxide, there are two signs of reaction. First a glow spreads through the mixture and, second, brown copper is seen at the end. The word-equation is:

COPPER OXIDE + IRON ⟶ COPPER + IRON OXIDE

So we can say that iron has a greater affinity for oxygen than has copper, but a lesser affinity for oxygen than has magnesium.

We now have the beginning of an **affinity series**, which we can build up by doing more experiments. In each of these a metal must be heated with the oxide of another metal, so that the two metals will compete for the oxygen. Some of these reactions are very violent, and you must only heat mixtures which your teacher recommends.

The experiments can be carried out on a crucible lid; but provided they are not too violent, it is often better to do them in test-tubes. Then the amount of oxygen is limited and the metal which loses its oxygen cannot be re-oxidised by reacting with the oxygen in the air. In either case the two powders must be thoroughly mixed, otherwise the oxygen cannot easily be transferred from one metal to the other. The evidence for reaction will usually be a red glow; also the products will usually differ in appearance from the reactants.

Some metals have very similar affinities for oxygen and experiments such as these cannot distinguish between them. The table (Table 9.1) shows the relative affinities of some metals for oxygen.

sodium, magnesium, aluminium	greatest affinity
zinc	↑
iron	
copper, lead	
silver, gold	least affinity

Table 9.1 A simple affinity series of metals for oxygen

9.3 Oxidation and reduction

As we saw in Chapter 5, the addition of oxygen is called **oxidation**. The removal of oxygen is called **reduction**. As an example, take the spectacular 'thermit' reaction:

ALUMINIUM + IRON OXIDE $\longrightarrow$ ALUMINIUM OXIDE + IRON

(Do not try this reaction yourself, ask your teacher to demonstrate it to you.)

The aluminium is *oxidized* to aluminium oxide and the iron oxide is *reduced* to iron. We also say that the iron oxide is the **oxidizing agent** (oxidant) since it supplies the oxygen which combines with the aluminium; the aluminium is the **reducing agent** (reductant) since it takes the oxygen away from the iron oxide.

Metals can reduce the oxides of metals which are below them in the affinity series, and metal oxides can be reduced by metals which are above them in the affinity series.

9.4 The position of carbon

If carbon is heated with copper oxide in a test-tube, a glow is seen in the mixture and brown copper is present at the end.

CARBON + COPPER OXIDE $\longrightarrow$ CARBON DIOXIDE + COPPER

The carbon has reduced the copper oxide to copper; if carbon is heated with magnesium oxide, no reaction occurs. Carbon must therefore be between magnesium and copper in the affinity series. Other experiments lead to carbon usually being placed just above iron in the series.

The word 'usually' in the last sentence is used because the position of carbon in the series depends on the temperature; above 800°C carbon is higher than iron and thus should reduce iron oxide. A good Bunsen burner will just about reach this temperature. In industry, where temperatures well over 1000°C can be reached, carbon can also reduce zinc oxide to zinc, a reaction which will not happen at the lower temperatures obtained with a Bunsen burner. There are two reasons why carbon is an important element for extracting metals from their ores: first it is cheap; second, the reaction produces carbon dioxide which is a gas and therefore easily got rid of, leaving just the solid metal (see also Section 13.2).

Metals above carbon in the series should reduce carbon dioxide. If a piece of burning magnesium is plunged into a gas jar of carbon dioxide it continues to glow, and white and black specks appear on the sides of the gas jar:

MAGNESIUM + CARBON DIOXIDE ⟶ MAGNESIUM OXIDE + CARBON
white   black

9.5 The displacement series

If an iron penknife blade is dipped in copper sulphate solution it becomes coated with copper. The iron is said to have **displaced** (pushed out) the copper from the copper sulphate. The word equation is:

IRON + COPPER SULPHATE ⟶ IRON SULPHATE + COPPER
solution   solution

If iron powder is shaken with copper sulphate solution, it is clear that a reaction has produced brown copper. Also the characteristic blue of the copper sulphate has been replaced by the very pale green (almost colourless) colour of iron sulphate. The result would be the same if copper chloride solution or copper nitrate solution were used. The reaction takes place with any soluble copper salt.

Other displacement reactions include:

1. COPPER + SILVER NITRATE ⟶ COPPER NITRATE + SILVER
solution   solution

If a copper wire is placed in silver nitrate solution, the solution turns blue because of the copper nitrate that is forming and grey needle-shaped crystals of silver are formed on the copper.

2. ZINC + LEAD NITRATE ⟶ ZINC NITRATE + LEAD
solution   solution

When a piece of zinc is placed in lead nitrate solution, crystals of lead begin to grow on it; this is excellent evidence

98

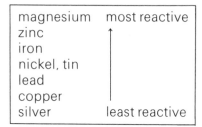

magnesium	most reactive
zinc	
iron	
nickel, tin	
lead	
copper	
silver	least reactive

Table 9.2 A displacement
series for metals

for a reaction, even though the solution does not change colour, since both the nitrates are colourless.

By placing metals in solutions of salts of other metals and seeing whether reactions occur it is possible to build up a **displacement series** (Table 9.2). Metals at the top will react with the solutions of salts of metals lower down, and the lower metal is displaced.

The displacement series is very similar to – but not exactly the same as – the affinity series. It can be used to separate some metals where experiments using oxides do not give satisfactory results (for example lead and copper). However, in some displacement experiments it is not easy to decide whether there is positive evidence of a reaction. For example, it is difficult to decide which is the higher of nickel and tin. In these cases the electrochemical series can be used (see Section 12.5).

Summary

1. Metals can be arranged in order of their affinity for oxygen in an **affinity series**. If a metal is heated with the oxide of a metal *below* it in the series, a reaction occurs, for example:

MAGNESIUM + COPPER OXIDE → MAGNESIUM OXIDE + COPPER

2. Oxidation is the addition of oxygen.
   Reduction is the removal of oxygen.
   Oxidizing agents (oxidants) oxidize other substances.
   Reducing agents (reductants) reduce other substances.

3. The non-metal carbon has a place in the affinity series which varies with temperature. Carbon is useful as an industrial reducing agent.

4. The **displacement series** is very similar to the affinity series. A metal high in the series will displace a metal *below* it from a solution of the lower metal's salt, for example:

COPPER + SILVER NITRATE → SILVER + COPPER NITRATE

Questions

1.† Some lead oxide was strongly heated in a crucible with some carbon and, on cooling, a small bead of metallic lead was found.

a. Is lead or carbon higher in the affinity series?
b. In the experiment, the lead oxide had been ....
c. In the experiment, the carbon had been ....

In a similar experiment there was found to be no reaction when zinc oxide and carbon were heated together.

d. Is zinc or carbon higher in the affinity series?
e. What conclusion can be drawn about the relative positions of zinc and lead in the affinity series?

2. When black copper oxide reacts with black carbon in a test-tube a shiny red-brown solid can be clearly seen once the tube has cooled.
a. What is the red-brown solid?
b. Write a 'word-equation' for this reaction.
c. How would you test for the gas that is formed?
d. When this reaction takes place on a crucible lid, very little of the red-brown solid can be seen at the end. Why is this?
e. What is meant by oxidation and reduction?
f. In this reaction which substance is oxidized and which is reduced?
g. Does carbon or copper have the greater affinity for oxygen?

3.[†] Give an explanation of the following.

When black copper oxide is heated with powdered charcoal (carbon) in a test-tube, the mixture glows and a brown solid is formed. However, when black copper oxide is heated with carbon on a crucible lid, the mixture glows, but little or no brown solid remains when the experiment is over.

4. Nickel does not react with zinc oxide.

Nickel reacts with lead oxide to form lead and nickel oxide.

a. Place the elements lead, nickel and zinc in order of their affinity for oxygen. (Most *reactive* first.)
b. What, if anything, would you expect to happen if you heated a mixture of zinc and lead oxide?
c. What, if anything, would you expect to happen if you heated a mixture of lead and zinc oxide?

5. When a piece of burning calcium is lowered into a gas jar of carbon dioxide, two solids, one white and one black, are formed.
a. What is the black solid?
b. What is the white solid?
c. The white solid is slightly soluble in water. What is the solution called?
d. Use this reaction to explain what is meant by oxidation and reduction.
e. Has carbon or calcium the greater affinity for oxygen?

6.
a. Why is carbon (coke) used to extract iron from iron ore (iron oxide)?
b. What else will be produced?
c. Why is carbon not used to extract aluminium from aluminium oxide?

7.†
a. Zinc is higher in the affinity series than copper. State what you would expect to see if:
  i A mixture of zinc powder and copper oxide is heated.
  ii A piece of copper foil is left immersed in zinc sulphate solution.

8. You are provided with a sample of an element X. Describe suitable experiments:
a. To find out whether it is a metal:
  i Using physical properties.
  ii Using chemical properties.
b. To find its position in the affinity series.

9.
a. Explain why an iron nail becomes pink-brown if placed in copper sulphate solution.
b. Explain why a piece of copper becomes pale grey when placed in silver nitrate solution. (The solution turns from colourless to blue.)
c. Place the metals copper, iron and silver in order of increasing reactivity.
d. What would you expect to happen if a piece of silver were dropped into iron sulphate solution?

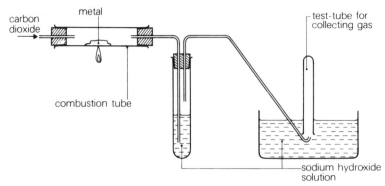

Fig 9.1

carbon dioxide

metal

test-tube for collecting gas

combustion tube

sodium hydroxide solution

10. (Difficult)

Zinc is more reactive than iron which is more reactive than tin.

a. Galvanized iron (iron coated with zinc) does not rust even when it is scratched. Why do you think that this is so?

b. Tin plate (iron coated with tin) rusts quite rapidly if the tin is scratched. Why is this?

11. (Difficult)

The apparatus shown in Fig 9.1 can be used to investigate the action of carbon dioxide on heated metals. The sodium hydroxide solution absorbs any excess carbon dioxide.

The experiment was first performed using magnesium.

a. Write a word-equation for the reaction which occurs.

b. Describe what you would *see* in the combustion tube when the magnesium reacted.

c. State with reasons whether you would expect any gas to be collected in the test-tube.

The experiment was repeated using zinc. A yellow residue (white when cool) was formed in the combustion tube and a gas collected in the test-tube. This gas burned with a blue flame and was not a zinc compound.

d. Say with reasons what the gas must be.

e. How could you test the gas to prove your conclusion in d.?

f. Write a word-equation for the reaction.

Chapter 10 **Hydrogen and water**

10.1 Obtaining hydrogen from acids

In Section 7.3 we found that acids were substances containing hydrogen, and we gave them alternative names:
hydrogen chloride for hydrochloric acid;
hydrogen sulphate for sulphuric acid;
hydrogen nitrate for nitric acid.
It is possible to *displace* hydrogen from acids in the same way as we displaced metals from their salts (Section 9.5). For example, if sulphuric acid is added to zinc powder in a test-tube, fizzing is seen. The reaction can be written:

ZINC + HYDROGEN SULPHATE $\longrightarrow$ HYDROGEN + ZINC SULPHATE
sulphuric acid

The test for hydrogen is that it explodes with a 'squeaky pop' when it is lit in the presence of oxygen. Collect the gas in a second test-tube placed over the tube in which the reaction is taking place (Fig 10.1). After a few moments, remove the lower tube and very quickly place a lighted splint at the mouth of the upper tube. The 'pop' should be heard, but only if you have been quick enough – the hydrogen escapes rapidly.

It is possible to place hydrogen in the displacement series by discovering which metals react with dilute acids to displace hydrogen. It is found that iron and the metals above will react, but lead, copper and others below them will not. Thus we can place hydrogen between iron and lead in the series.

These experiments add something to our understanding of the word 'acid'. We can now define an acid as a substance

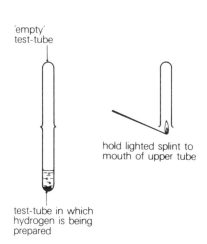

'empty' test-tube

hold lighted splint to mouth of upper tube

test-tube in which hydrogen is being prepared

Fig 10.1 Testing for hydrogen

103

containing hydrogen which can be displaced by a reactive metal.

The general reaction between acids and the metals above hydrogen in the displacement series can be written:

METAL + ACID ⟶ HYDROGEN + SALT

for example:

MAGNESIUM + HYDROGEN CHLORIDE ⟶ HYDROGEN + MAGNESIUM CHLORIDE
hydrochloric acid

IRON + HYDROGEN SULPHATE ⟶ HYDROGEN + IRON SULPHATE

Nitric acid has some unusual properties and does not always react in the same way as the other acids.

10.2 The laboratory preparation of hydrogen

The apparatus shown in Fig 10.2 can be used to prepare hydrogen in the laboratory. Since a steady supply is needed, larger pieces of zinc (called **granulated** zinc) are used, though the reaction is often rather too slow until some copper sulphate solution is added to speed it up. The hydrogen is collected 'over water', as shown in the diagram.

The first tubes collected may not explode at all when they are lit since they contain almost all air, pushed out of the flask by the hydrogen. Later tubes will produce a 'pop' when lit as they contain a mixture of hydrogen and air. Eventually tubes will burn much more quietly, as pure hydrogen burns steadily in air, but hydrogen–air mixtures explode when lit. Because of this many serious accidents have occurred in school laboratories with the apparatus shown in Fig 10.2. The gas must **never** be ignited at the end of the delivery tube until it is certain that all the air has been pushed out of the flask, otherwise an explosion will occur there. To ensure that all the air has been pushed out, tubes of hydrogen should be collected and tested until they burn steadily. The jet must then be lit *only* from the hydrogen burning in the test-tube.

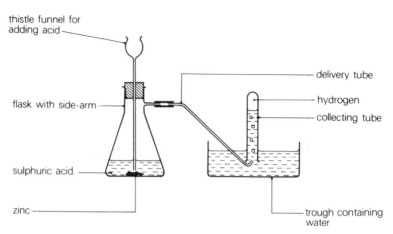

thistle funnel for adding acid

delivery tube

hydrogen

flask with side-arm

collecting tube

sulphuric acid

zinc

trough containing water

Fig 10.2 The preparation of hydrogen

This should only be done by a teacher. It is safer to use a hydrogen cylinder if a burning jet of hydrogen is required (as in Section 10.3).

The gas which has been collected can be seen to be colourless and it has no smell. The fact that it is less dense than air can be demonstrated by placing a test-tube above a tube of gas (Fig 10.3a) and one below a tube of gas (Fig 10.3b). In the first case both tubes will pop when tested, but in Fig 10.3b only the top tube will pop.

10.3 Water – the oxide of hydrogen

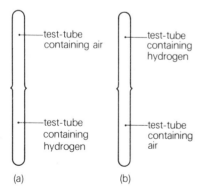

test-tube containing air

test-tube containing hydrogen

test-tube containing hydrogen

test-tube containing air

(a)　　　　　(b)

Fig 10.3 The density of hydrogen

In Chapter 5 (Section 5.5) we *assumed* that water was the oxide of hydrogen, so we ought to look at an experiment which *proves* this. The apparatus shown in Fig 10.4 may be used.

If the hydrogen is obtained from the previous experiment, it must be dried to remove the water vapour which comes from the dilute sulphuric acid. Anhydrous calcium chloride is a good general-purpose drying agent which may be used here. The gas can be lit at the jet **only after taking the precautions described above**, but it is much safer to use a hydrogen cylinder to supply the dry gas. **You should**

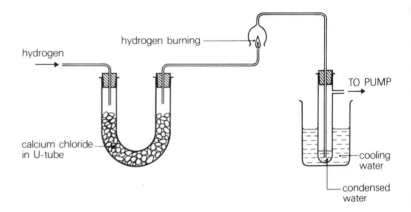

hydrogen burning

hydrogen

TO PUMP

calcium chloride
in U-tube

cooling
water

condensed
water

Fig 10.4 Burning hydrogen

never try this experiment for yourself because of the
danger of an explosion.

The liquid which collects can be shown to be water by the
usual tests (see Section 3.6) the most important being that it
boils near 100°C and freezes at 0°C.

10.4 The reaction of metals with water and steam

Some of the most reactive metals will react with cold water.
For example:

potassium moves around on a water surface, fizzes and
catches fire. The water becomes alkaline;

sodium moves around on a water surface and fizzes, but it
does not catch fire unless its movement is restricted. The
water becomes alkaline;

calcium sinks, as it is denser than water, and starts reacting
slowly, then more vigorously. A white cloudiness develops
in the water and it becomes alkaline.

In each of these the reaction is the same:

METAL + WATER ⟶ METAL HYDROXIDE + HYDROGEN

Sodium and potassium hydroxides are soluble and their
presence can be detected by the alkalinity of the solution.
Calcium hydroxide is less soluble and forms the white
cloudiness. It is rather dangerous to try to collect the

hydrogen in the reactions of sodium and potassium, but the reaction between calcium and water can be done in a test-tube and the presence of hydrogen can easily be shown.

These experiments show that the three metals are above hydrogen in the affinity series, since they reduce its oxide (remove the oxygen from water). It can also be seen that the metals have an *order* of reactivity: potassium (most reactive) then sodium, then calcium. These three elements are at the top of the affinity series.

The next metal in the affinity series, magnesium, will react very slowly with water, even if it is heated. But it will react readily with steam. The apparatus of Fig 10.5a can be used. The metal should be heated first and the Bunsen then flicked down to drive some steam from the mineral wool. This requires much less heat, and a common mistake is to drive off all the steam before the metal is hot enough to react.

The reaction of magnesium is rather too fast for the hydrogen to be collected, but it can be lit at the end of the tube A. Zinc and iron (being lower in the affinity series) react more slowly with steam, and the hydrogen can be collected 'over water' (Fig 10.5b).

In each case the reaction is:

METAL + STEAM ⟶ METAL OXIDE + HYDROGEN
hydrogen oxide

The oxides of the metals can be seen in the test-tubes after the reaction.

Metals below iron in the affinity series will not react with steam, so we can say that hydrogen comes just below iron in

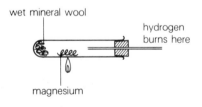

(a)

Fig 10.5 The action of steam on metals

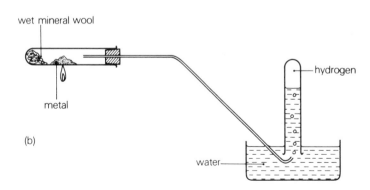

(b)

the affinity series, as it does in the displacement series (Section 10.1). The affinity series is given in Appendix 3.

10.5 Reduction of metal oxides with hydrogen

Since hydrogen is above copper and lead in the affinity series it can be used to reduce their oxides. The apparatus of Fig 10.6a can be used.

Hydrogen (from a cylinder) is passed over the heated metal oxide and the excess is burned off at the small hole. Black copper oxide turns to brown copper which will conduct electricity. Yellow lead oxide turns grey, and shiny globules of molten lead are seen. The equation for both reactions is:

METAL OXIDE + HYDROGEN ⟶ METAL + STEAM
hydrogen oxide

If the apparatus shown in Fig 10.6b is used, water can be condensed out from the hot gases produced and tested as in Section 3.6.

Summary
1. Metals above hydrogen in the affinity series react with hydrochloric acid and sulphuric acid like this:

METAL + ACID ⟶ HYDROGEN + SALT

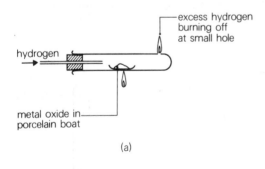

(a)

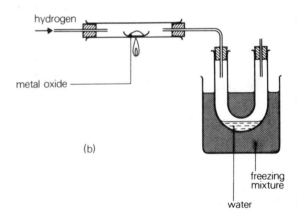

(b)

Fig 10.6 The action of hydrogen on metal oxides

This reaction can be used to prepare hydrogen in the laboratory.

2. Hydrogen burns to form water. **Great care must be taken** because hydrogen explodes when mixed with air or oxygen. Small explosions are heard in the 'pop' test for hydrogen.

3. Metals high in the affinity series react with water like this:

METAL + WATER $\longrightarrow$ METAL HYDROXIDE + HYDROGEN

Metals lower in the affinity series (but still above hydrogen) react with *steam*:

METAL + STEAM $\longrightarrow$ METAL OXIDE + HYDROGEN

4. Hydrogen will reduce the oxides of metals which are below it in the affinity series:

METAL OXIDE + HYDROGEN $\longrightarrow$ METAL + STEAM

Questions

1. Sketch the apparatus you would use to prepare hydrogen:

a. From zinc and dilute sulphuric acid.

b. From zinc and steam.

2.

a. When hydrogen burns with a pop, what is formed?

b. Why does impure hydrogen often burn with a loud pop, while pure hydrogen often burns without making a noise?

c. When hydrogen is prepared in a large apparatus it must always be collected *before* it is tested. Why is it dangerous to try to light the hydrogen as it comes out of the apparatus?

3.

a. Why can hydrogen *not* be made from copper and sulphuric acid?

b. What products are formed when hydrogen is passed over heated copper oxide?

c. Sketch the apparatus you would use in b.

d. What would you see during the experiment?

e. What would you see if you used lead oxide instead of copper oxide?

f. What would you see if you used calcium oxide instead of copper oxide?

g. How would you make hydrogen? (Assume you have no cylinder!)

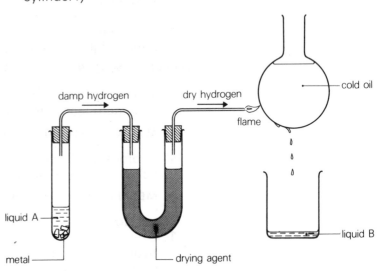

Fig 10.7

4.† In Fig 10.7 damp hydrogen gas is produced in the tube on the left. It is completely dried by passing through the U-tube containing the drying agent, and it is burnt as it comes out of the tube on the right very near a large flask containing cold oil. Liquid B is found to be dripping from the bottom of the large flask.

a. In order to make hydrogen in this way, suggest:
   i What the metal might be.
   ii What liquid A might be.

b. Name a metal which would *not* be suitable for this experiment.

c. Suggest a substance which could be used as a drying agent.

d. What is liquid B?

e. How is liquid B formed?

f. What change would there be in the flame if powdered metal were used?

5.† The apparatus shown in Fig 10.8 is used for making and collecting hydrogen.

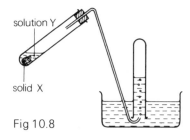

solution Y

solid X

Fig 10.8

a. Name one pair of substances, X and Y, which might be used in the apparatus.
b. The first test-tube of gas collected from the above apparatus may be somewhat different from the rest. Why is this so?
c. What test would you use to show that the gas collected was hydrogen?
d. Why is hydrogen sometimes used in balloons?
e. What change would you expect to see in black copper oxide if it were heated in a tube and hydrogen passed over it?
f. Name the solid product in e.
g. Nothing happens when hydrogen is passed over heated magnesium oxide. Explain why this is so.

6. Using the apparatus in Fig 10.6b, it is possible to condense the water.
a. How has the water formed?
b. Name two physical tests to show that the liquid was water.
c. Name two chemical tests to show that the liquid was water.
d. Someone suggests that the water could have been condensed from the air. How would you prevent water from the air getting in?

7.† When hydrogen is passed over gently heated aluminium oxide, nothing is observed to happen. When hydrogen is passed over gently heated copper oxide, a red glow spreads through the solid, drops of condensed moisture are seen and afterwards a reddish powder is left which conducts electricity.
  i What do you conclude about hydrogen being more or less active than aluminium or copper?
  ii Account for the observations made in the case of the copper oxide.

8.† Read carefully the following information about three solids, and then answer the questions.
Solid X – did not react when heated in steam, but when it was heated in hydrogen, water was formed and the solid lost mass.

Solid Y – did not react with either steam or hydrogen even on strong heating.

Solid Z – did not react when heated in hydrogen, but when heated in steam hydrogen was formed and the solid gained mass.

a. Why is solid X not a metallic element?
b. Why is solid X not magnesium?
c. Explain how it is possible for a substance to gain in mass when heated in steam.
d. Why is solid Z not gold?
e. Name solids which could fit the description of solids X, Y and Z.

9.[†] The following is an affinity (activity) series, written in order of decreasing reactivity:

magnesium, carbon, iron, hydrogen, copper.

In each of the following cases state what products, if any, you would expect to obtain on heating these pairs of substances together.

a. Magnesium + carbon dioxide.
b. Iron + steam.
c. Copper + iron oxide.

10.[†] Imagine that the bottles of copper oxide and powdered carbon in a laboratory have lost their labels. They are both black powders. It is necessary to find out which of the bottles contains which substance.

Describe in detail two experiments by which you could make quite sure which bottle contains which substance.

11.[†] In an experiment to investigate the reaction of magnesium in dilute hydrochloric acid, a chemist took several 2 cm lengths of magnesium ribbon and placed them in equal volumes of acid of different concentrations. He measured the time taken for the magnesium to disappear and obtained the results shown in Fig 10.9.

a. How long would it take for 2 cm of ribbon to disappear in 3% acid?
b. If the concentration of acid is doubled, what is the effect on the time taken for the magnesium to disappear?

Fig 10.9

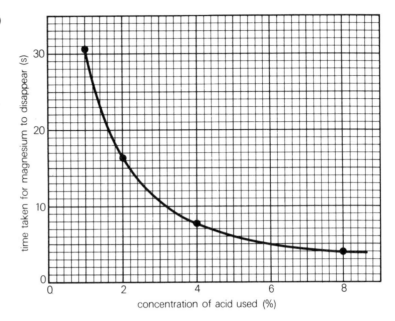

c. When the chemist used acid of less than 1% concentration the reaction became very slow and eventually stopped, leaving some of the magnesium. Explain why the reaction stopped.

d. The chemist recorded in his observations that a piece of ribbon that had been stored for a long time did not fizz much for the first few seconds after it was put into the acid. Why do you think this was so?

e. Suggest one factor the chemist might vary in his further investigation of this reaction.

12. (Difficult)
When dilute nitric acid is added to copper a brown gas is given off and the solution turns blue.

a. The gas is an oxide. Which oxide is it? (Refer back to Chapter 6 if you need help.)

b. Which element might be in the blue solution? (Think of other blue solutions.)

c. What do you think the blue solution might be?

d. Do you think hydrogen was given off as well as the brown gas?

13. (Difficult)

Some pupils heated samples from bottles labelled 'black copper oxide' in a stream of hydrogen until no further change occurred. They weighed the black solid before heating and the residue which remained after heating.

Here are their results:

Sample	Mass of black solid	Mass of residue
A	3.6 g	2.4 g
B	6.4 g	5.1 g
C	4.3 g	3.4 g
D	4.7 g	4.3 g
E	7.6 g	5.2 g
F	8.9 g	7.1 g

The samples came from three different bottles and it was suggested that some of the bottles contained impurities. Pure copper oxide contains 80% by mass of copper.

a. Plot a graph of 'mass of residue' against 'mass of black solid' (horizontal axis).

b. Use the graph to identify which samples came from which of the three different bottles.

c. Did any of the bottles contain pure copper oxide? Explain your reasoning.

d. Suggest the kinds of impurities which might have been present in the other bottles.

Chapter 11 **Analysis of simple salts**

11.1 What are salts?

We first met salts in Chapter 7 (Section 7.3) where we found that they were the product of neutralization reactions. Salts can be recognized from their names; the first part is the name of a metal, the second is a name based on a non-metal. Thus copper sulphate, copper chloride and copper nitrate are all **copper salts**. The same 'non-metal parts', sulphate, chloride and nitrate will go with sodium to make a series of sodium salts, and so on. The commonest 'non-metal parts' are: bromide, carbonate, chloride, iodide, nitrate, phosphate sulphide and sulphate. Remember those ending in -*ide* contain one non-metal only; thus sodium sulph*ide* is a compound which contains just sodium and sulphur. Those ending in -*ate* contain the non-metal and *oxygen*. Thus sodium sulph*ate* contains sodium, sulphur and oxygen.

Salts are found dissolved in the sea, in rocks and in evaporated deposits. One of the chemist's jobs is to find out the composition of substances, that is which elements they contain. The process is called **analysis** and this Chapter is about some of the simpler ways in which salts can be analysed.

11.2 Some preliminary tests

Before testing for one or other metal or non-metal, a chemist wants to be able to do some general tests to give him some idea of what a substance might be. These tests are:
1. **Appearance.**
   The colour of a salt often tells us something about the

metal part, for example:
copper salts are blue or green;
iron salts are green or brown.

2. **The action of heat in a dry test-tube.**
   To the trained eye this test can reveal a lot about a substance. Some simple results are:

a. Colour change,
   for example: if lead is present the residue will be orange when hot and yellow when cold;
   if zinc is present the residue will be yellow when hot and white when cold.

b. A gas is evolved:
   carbon dioxide from a *carbonate*;
   water vapour from a *hydrated salt.*

3. **Is it soluble in water?**
   To perform this test, shake very little of the solid with half a test-tube of water. Do not expect a great heap of powder to dissolve!

   Here are some simple rules:
   all *sodium* and *potassium* salts are soluble;
   all *nitrates* are soluble;
   all *chlorides* are soluble except lead chloride and silver chloride;
   all *sulphates* are soluble except barium sulphate and lead sulphate;
   all *carbonates* are *insoluble* except those of sodium and potassium.

4. **Action of dilute acid.**
   If dilute hydrochloric acid is added to certain salts, gases are evolved. The most usual is *carbon dioxide* from a *carbonate.*

11.3 Tests for the 'metal part'

Some idea of the nature of the metal may have been obtained from preliminary tests, particularly if the metal has coloured salts. However, a **flame test** is always worth doing as it is a quick and easy way of distinguishing between many metals.

potassium	lilac (pale mauve)
sodium	*intense* yellow (pale yellow is probably due to small sodium impurity)
calcium	red
barium	apple green
lead	blue
copper	blue-green (with white flashes)

Table 11.1 Flame colours of some common metals

To carry out a flame test, a **nichrome** wire is used. This is made of a nickel–chromium alloy which does not have a flame colour of its own. The wire is dipped in concentrated hydrochloric acid in a watch glass and then placed in the *side* of a roaring Bunsen flame (not the blue cone). This is repeated until no flame colour is seen. The wire is then dipped in the acid again and into the sample to be tested. A little sticks to the moistened wire and is carried to the flame. If a colour is not developed it is best to return the wire to the acid rather than to the solid before placing it in the flame again. Eventually a flame colour is often seen and this identifies the metals shown in Table 11.1. The colour is given by *all* salts of the metal concerned. The concentrated acid converts them all to the chlorides which vaporize well in the flame.

The commonest metals which do not have a flame colour are magnesium, zinc and iron. Iron can often be recognized by the colour of its compounds (green or brown) and zinc by the colour of the residue after heating the salt (yellow when hot, white when cold). Magnesium has no coloured compounds and a special reagent is needed to help identify it, called magneson 1. The suspected magnesium salt is dissolved in water and a few drops of magneson 1 are added, followed by an equal volume of dilute sodium hydroxide solution. If magnesium is present, a blue precipitate* will develop in the pink solution. This test should be carried out only if other metals have been shown to be absent since some of them might also give a similar precipitate.

11.4 Tests for the 'non-metal part'

There is no general test for the non-metal part similar to the flame-test for metals, so we will restrict ourselves to identifying carbonate, sulphate and chloride.

Carbonate will already have been identified in the preliminary test with hydrochloric acid. If carbonate is not

*A precipitate is a solid substance which is formed when two clear solutions are mixed.

present, the salt should be dissolved in dilute nitric acid and divided into two parts.

a. Test one part with silver nitrate solution. If a white precipitate of insoluble silver chloride is formed it indicates that the salt is a *chloride*.

b. Test the other part with barium chloride solution. If a white precipitate of insoluble barium sulphate is formed it indicates that the salt is a *sulphate*.

There is no simple test for the other common non-metal part which is *nitrate*.

11.5 Summary of methods of analysis

A 'flow diagram' which summarizes the previous sections is given in Table 11.2. Much more complicated schemes are available to more advanced chemists, but at every level the good analytical chemist is one who keeps his eyes (and nose) open and thinks about what he observes, rather than just plodding through the scheme.

11.6 Malachite

This green substance, which is found in rocks in central Africa, is said to be the **ore** of a common metal. (The ore of a metal is a compound of that metal which occurs naturally in the earth.) The analysis of crushed, purified malachite provides a good chance to use some of the chemistry we have studied up to now.

If the preliminary tests are carried out on crushed malachite, the results are:

appearance – a green solid;
action of heat – solid turns black, carbon dioxide is evolved;
solubility – insoluble in water;
action of dilute sulphuric acid – powder fizzes, carbon dioxide is evolved, a blue solution is left.

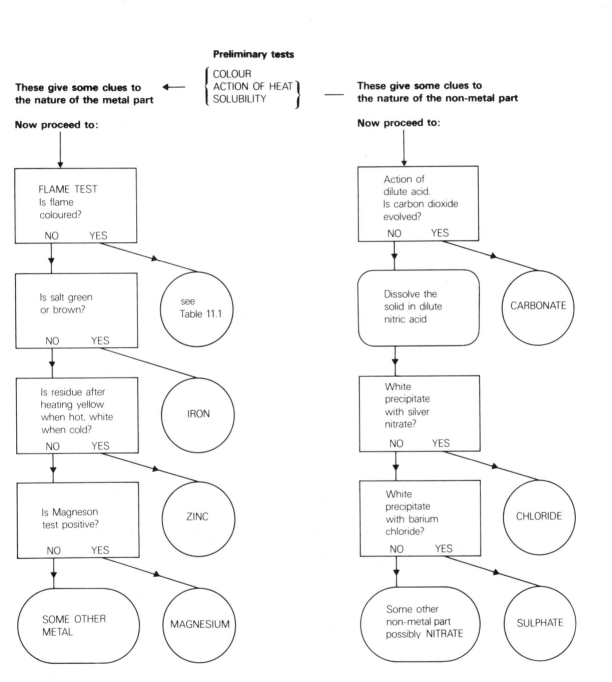

Table 11.2 A flow diagram for simple analysis

These tests tell us a lot about malachite. We see clearly that the non-metal part is carbonate since carbon dioxide is given off on heating and on the addition of acid.

The metal part is probably copper, as the colours blue and green indicate. More tests can be done to make sure of this. The flame test gives a blue-green colour which again indicates copper. How can copper be extracted from the solid to make certain? There are at least four ways of doing this:

1. **Reduction with carbon.**

   The black solid which remains after heating is probably copper oxide and this can be reduced with powdered carbon (charcoal) by heating in a test-tube. Brown copper can be seen at the end (Section 9.4).

2. **Reduction with hydrogen.**

   The black solid can also be reduced using hydrogen (Section 10.5). Since water, the other product, is given off as a vapour, the copper which remains can be tested to show that it conducts electricity.

3. **Displacement with iron.**

   The solution which remains after the addition of sulphuric acid is copper sulphate solution. If we dip an iron nail into this it will *displace* copper from the solution (Section 9.5) and become coated brown.

4. **Electrolysis.**

   The blue solution can also be electrolysed and copper is deposited at the cathode (Chapter 12).

The reactions of malachite are summarized in Table 11.3.

11.7 Limestone

Limestone is another rock which can be dug out of the ground. It also is the ore of a metal.

The preliminary tests on powdered limestone give the following results:

appearance – a white powder;
action of heat – no apparent reaction;
solubility – insoluble in water;
action of dilute hydrochloric acid – fizzing seen, carbon dioxide is evolved, a colourless solution remains.

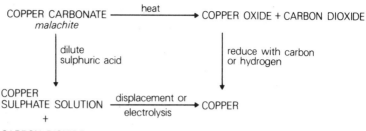

COPPER CARBONATE —— heat ——→ COPPER OXIDE + CARBON DIOXIDE
malachite

| dilute sulphuric acid

reduce with carbon or hydrogen

COPPER
SULPHATE SOLUTION —— displacement or electrolysis ——→ COPPER
+
CARBON DIOXIDE

Table 11.3 The reactions of malachite

The action of acid indicates that a carbonate is present, so it is strange that carbon dioxide is not evolved on heating. In fact the carbonates of the most reactive metals do not decompose to give carbon dioxide except at high temperatures. However, it is found to be possible to decompose a lump of limestone by holding it in tongs and heating it in the hottest part of a Bunsen flame (just above the blue cone) for five minutes. The residue *looks* similar to the limestone we started with, though it is possibly a little more crumbly. It is not possible to catch the carbon dioxide when heating in this way so we must look for other signs that a reaction has occurred. These are:

1. Addition of acid to part of the residue should not give any fizzing, though this depends on whether the solid has been heated completely enough.
2. If water is added in drops to the lump which remains, there is a reaction. The lump expands and cracks, heat is given out, and the lump absorbs the first few drops of water without becoming damp. This does not happen when water is added to the limestone chip before it is heated.

These results show that there has been a *reaction*. More useful information can be gained from further experiments on the white solid obtained by adding water to the residue after heating. If this solid is shaken with distilled water it does not appear to be very soluble. However, if the solution is filtered, the pH of the filtrate is found to be alkaline, so some of the solid must have dissolved. If carbon dioxide is blown through the solution, a milkiness appears.

The last solution obviously resembles limewater, which is calcium hydroxide solution. A flame test on any of these solids will give a red flame, so we can tell they are calcium compounds.

We can therefore write:

CALCIUM CARBONATE $\longrightarrow$ RESIDUE + CARBON $\xrightarrow{\text{water}}$ CALCIUM HYDROXIDE
(limestone)   DIOXIDE

The residue is fairly clearly calcium oxide, since copper carbonate gives copper oxide when heated. We also know that alkaline oxides react with water to form hydroxides (Section 7.3).

A summary of the reactions is shown in Table 11.4. It should be remembered that the milkiness in limewater is calcium carbonate, so that we can go full circle, as shown. Included in the flow diagram are the common names for the materials, and it will be noticed that calcium carbonate occurs in nature not only as **limestone**, but as **marble**, **chalk**, **Iceland spar** and **calcite**.

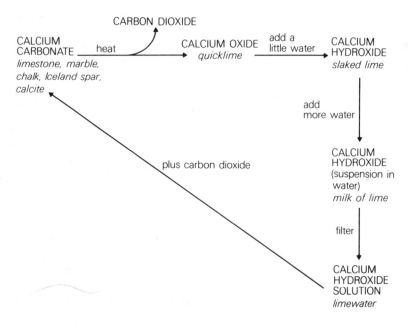

Table 11.4 The reactions of limestone

Questions

1. The ore, chalcanthite, is blue. It dissolves in water and in acids. It does not fizz with acids.

a. When an iron nail is dropped into a chalcanthite solution, the nail goes red-brown. Which metal does chalcanthite contain?

b. If chalcanthite does *not* fizz with acids, which 'non-metal part' does it not contain?

c. Chalcanthite solution forms a white precipitate with acidified barium chloride solution. Which 'non-metal part' does chalcanthite contain?

d. What is the chemical name of chalcanthite?

e. Chalcanthite can be found at Rio Tinto in Spain. Do you think it is likely that it is found at the surface or is it found underground? Give a reason for your answer.

2. At the Strassfurt salt mines in Germany, large deposits of sylvite are found. Sylvite is white and it dissolves in water.

a. Sylvite gives a lilac flame. Which metal does it contain?

b. Sylvite does not fizz with acids nor does its solution form a precipitate with acidified barium chloride solution. Which 'non-metal parts' does sylvite *not* contain?

c. Sylvite solution forms a white precipitate with acidified silver nitrate solution. What 'non-metal part' does sylvite contain?

d. What is the chemical name of sylvite?

3. X, Y and Z are the white carbonates of calcium, sodium and zinc (though not necessarily in that order).

a. How would you show that X, Y and Z are carbonates?

b. X and Y were almost insoluble in water, while Z was soluble and alkaline. When heated, Y decomposed with great difficulty while X decomposed readily to give a yellow solid, which became white again as it cooled. Use this information to identify X, Y and Z.

4.[†] A small sample of a powdered mineral was heated strongly (in the absence of air) in a hard glass test-tube fitted with a delivery tube dipping into limewater. The limewater soon turned milky. A black solid found in the test-tube dissolved in dilute sulphuric acid giving a pale blue solution which gradually lost its colour when a weighed iron nail was dipped into it. Meanwhile, a pink deposit formed on the iron nail.

a. Name three elements that are certainly present in the mineral.
b. What two elements are likely to be present in the black solid?
c. Why do you think the blue solution lost its colour?
d. If the pink deposit were scraped off the nail and the latter reweighed, would you expect any change in weight? If so, would you expect an increase or a decrease?
e. How would you attempt to turn the pink deposit back to the black solid?

5. When limestone is heated it forms quicklime (see Table 11.4).
a. How would the mass of quicklime compare with the mass of limestone?
b. Is the slaking of quicklime with a drop of water a mixing process or a chemical reaction? Give reasons for your answer.
c. How would you try to reconvert slaked lime into quicklime?
d. How would you try to reconvert quicklime into calcium carbonate?

6. Read the following passage carefully.
   Metal A reacts readily with water to give a colourless gas B and a milky sludge. Filtration of the sludge gives a white solid and a colourless solution C.
   The gas B can be trapped in an upside down test-tube and burns in air, forming a small amount of a colourless liquid D.
   The solution C goes milky when carbon dioxide is bubbled through it.
a. Use the above information to suggest a possible name for each substance A to D.
b. Explain the reasons for your answers.
c. How would you show that A is a metal (without destroying it)?
d. What would you expect the pH of solution C to be? Give a reason for your answer.

7. Magnesium carbonate (magnesite) decomposes more easily into a gas and another solid than calcium carbonate (calcite, limestone) does.

a. What gas and white solid would you get from magnesite?
b. The solid is less soluble than calcium oxide and forms a suspension in water that looks like 'milk of lime'. What name do you think is given to this suspension?
c. What medical use does this suspension have?
d. How would you expect magnesite to react with acids?

8. The white ore, witherite, fizzes when dilute hydrochloric acid is added. A gas is given off that turns limewater milky.
a. What is the gas?
b. What is the 'non-metal part' in witherite?
c. A flame test on witherite produces an apple-green flame. What is the 'metal part' in witherite?
d. What is the chemical name of witherite?
e. After witherite is treated with dilute hydrochloric acid, the solution forms a white precipitate when sulphuric acid is added. What is this precipitate? (This last part is difficult.)

9. When a sample of clear sea water is evaporated, different crystals form at different stages of the evaporation.

	Amount of evaporation	Metal part tests	Non-metal part tests
P	0–60%	red flame	carbon dioxide with acid
Q	80–85%	red flame	white solid with barium chloride
R	90–95%	intense yellow flame	white solid with silver nitrate
S	98–99%	no flame, but blue solid with magneson 1	white solid with barium chloride

a. What are the four salts P, Q, R and S?
b. Of the four which is the most soluble in water and which the least?

c. The amount of R in the sea far exceeds the amount of the other salts together. Does this surprise you?
d. The solution that remains after 99% evaporation gives a lilac flame colour. What does this tell you?
e. Some seas evaporate and then salt deposits form. Different salts often occur in different places on the old sea-bed. Suggest a reason for this.

10. 25 cm³ each of samples of different sorts of water were added to beakers. The samples were then evaporated to dryness. The solid that was left in each beaker was then weighed.

Type of water	Mass of beaker	Mass of beaker and solid left after evaporation
sea water	22.75 g	23.67 g
'hard' tap water	23.08 g	23.19 g
'softened' tap water	21.90 g	21.99 g
'deionized' water	22.44 g	22.44 g

a. How much solid was left in each case?
b. How pure do you think 'deionized' water is?
c. Is 'softened' tap water pure? Give a reason for your answer.
d. How much solid would you expect to get if you evaporated distilled water?
e. How much solid would you expect to get if you evaporated rain water?

11. (Difficult)
A blue solid A gives off steam and two other gases when heated. They are B, a brown acidic gas, and C, a colourless gas which relights a glowing splint. A black residue D remains after heating. When D is added to nitric acid, a blue solution of A is obtained. An iron nail placed in this solution soon becomes coated with a brown substance E.
a. Identify the gas C.
b. What can you say about the black solid D knowing that it reacts with nitric acid as stated?

c. What can you say about the compound A knowing that it is formed by the action of nitric acid on D?
d. State, with reasons, the elements you think are present in the gas B.
e. State, with reasons, the nature of E and explain how it is formed.
f. Name A and show the above reactions in the form of a flow diagram.

Background reading

The hardness of water
Water is said to be 'hard' when it does not form a 'lather' (bubbles) with soap. Instead, a white precipitate (called scum) is formed. No lather forms until all the hardness has been removed by the soap and this is a waste of soap. Also the scum tends to grind into clothes when they are being washed, causing damage. Hardness is caused by calcium or magnesium salts dissolved in the water. There are two types of hardness.

Temporary hardness is caused by the presence of calcium hydrogencarbonate or magnesium hydrogencarbonate in solution. It is called temporary because these salts are removed by boiling the water. The hydrogencarbonates get into the water by a reaction which occurs when rainwater flows over limestone rocks. Rainwater contains dissolved carbon dioxide and limestone is calcium carbonate (Section 11.7).
The reaction is:

CALCIUM CARBONATE + WATER + CARBON DIOXIDE ⟶ CALCIUM HYDROGENCARBONATE
(soluble)

You can see this reaction occurring if you continue to pass carbon dioxide through calcium hydroxide solution for a long time. The milky precipitate of calcium carbonate which forms at first (Section 11.7) *redissolves* to give calcium hydrogencarbonate and the solution goes clear again.

On boiling the reaction is reversed and carbonates are precipitated. Thus the hardness is removed. However, this is the cause of 'fur' in kettles and scale in boilers and pipes

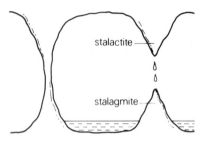

stalactite

stalagmite

Fig 11.1 Stalactites and stalagmites

which can be a nuisance. (It can also be dangerous if the pipes become completely blocked.)

Calcium hydrogencarbonate also turns back to calcium carbonate when temporarily hard water is evaporated. This is the cause of stalactites and stalagmites in limestone caves. The water (containing calcium hydrogencarbonate) drips down very slowly and much of it evaporates either at the top (forming a stalactite) or at the bottom (forming a stalagmite). Thus both stalagmites and stalactites are made of calcium carbonate (Fig 11.1).

Permanent hardness is caused by other calcium or magnesium salts, such as sulphates and chlorides. These are present in certain rocks and dissolve in water which passes over them. These salts are not decomposed by boiling.

Water may be softened by several processes, but the commonest is known as 'ion exchange'. Hard water is passed through a water softener which turns the calcium and magnesium salts into sodium salts. These do not cause hardness as they do not form a scum with soap.

Questions
1. Summarize the disadvantages of hard water. Can you think of any advantages?
2. How could you show that water which had passed through a water softener contained sodium salts but no longer any calcium or magnesium salts?
3. A method of measuring hardness is to add soap solution to a water sample in small portions. After the addition of a portion of soap, the mixture is shaken. When all the hardness has been removed by the soap, a 'permanent lather' is formed, that is bubbles which last for at least one minute. The amount of soap added is a measure of the hardness.

    If you were given various samples of water, describe experiments by which you could measure their relative hardness. How could you find out how much of the hardness of a sample was permanent and how much temporary?

Chapter 12 **Electricity and chemistry**

12.1 Which substances conduct electricity?

To test whether substances conduct electricity we need an electrical circuit. This must contain a **power supply** (battery or powerpack), a means of detecting whether a **current** is flowing (ammeter or light bulb) and the sample, all joined by wires. This is represented in Fig 12.1. If the sample conducts electricity, the bulb will light.

Solids can be tested by fastening the crocodile clips on to either side of a lump of material. As we saw in Chapter 8, metals and carbon conduct electricity. Non-metals and solids which are compounds do not.

Liquids and *solutions* can be tested by dipping a pair of carbon rods into them (Fig 12.2). It is found that no pure substances which are liquids at room temperature conduct electricity (with the exception of the liquid metal, mercury).

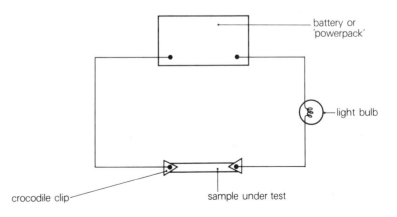

Fig 12.1 Testing the conductivity of a solid

battery or 'powerpack'

light bulb

crocodile clip

sample under test

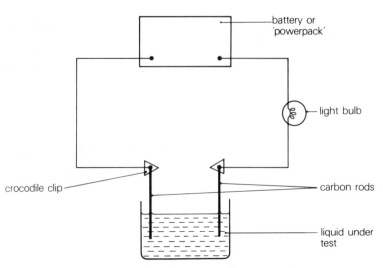

battery or 'powerpack'

light bulb

crocodile clip

carbon rods

liquid under test

Fig 12.2 Testing the conductivity of
a liquid or a solution

It may come as a surprise to you to discover that pure water
is a poor conductor. However, many *solutions* conduct, and
water, as it occurs in nature, is seldom very pure.

It is found that solutions in water of *salts*, *acids* and *alkalis*
conduct electricity. Solutions in water of other substances,
such as ethanol or sugar do not conduct. When the carbon
rods are dipped into solutions which do conduct, bubbling is
seen. The solutions are being broken down by the electricity,
a process called **electrolysis**.

Molten salts also conduct electricity and this can be
shown by melting the salt in a crucible and dipping in the
carbon rods. It is just possible to melt calcium chloride and
potassium iodide with a good Bunsen in order to try this.
Again the electricity **decomposes** the salts to their
elements (brown iodine is seen, for example, when
potassium iodide conducts). We shall investigate the
products of the decomposition in the next section.

We have seen that metals conduct without being broken
down, but all other substances which conduct decompose
as they do so. These are called **electrolytes** and are said to
undergo electrolysis when a current passes through them.

Summary
Solids   metals and carbon conduct (without electrolysis)
           other solids do not conduct

Liquids   molten metals conduct (without electrolysis)
molten salts are electrolytes
other pure liquids do not conduct

Solutions   solutions of salts, acids and alkalis are
electrolytes
other solutions do not conduct

12.2 Electrolysis of molten salts

First we must consider the carbon rods, which are called
electrodes. The positive electrode (attached to the positive
terminal of the power supply) is called the **anode** and the
negative electrode is called the **cathode**.

Lead bromide is a salt which is easily melted. If the
apparatus shown in Fig 12.3 is used to electrolyse the
molten salt, a small metallic globule is seen at the cathode
and brown fumes at the anode. The metallic globule is lead
and the brown fumes are bromine. Thus the compound lead
bromide has been broken down into its elements by the
electricity. Some results for other similar electrolytes are
shown in Table 12.1.

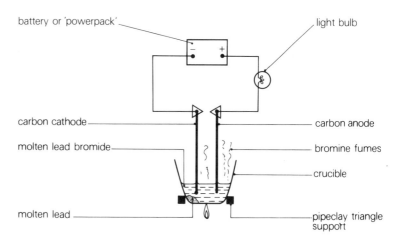

Fig 12.3 The electrolysis of molten
lead bromide

Substance	Cathode product	Anode product
molten sodium chloride	sodium (hard to see)	chlorine (smell, bleaches pH paper)
molten potassium iodide	potassium (hard to see)	iodine (brown colour, purple vapour)

Table 12.1 Electrolysis of two molten salts

When molten salts are electrolysed the *metal* is released at the *cathode* and the *non-metal* at the *anode*.

12.3 Electrolysis of solutions

In Section 12.1 it was stated that bubbles were seen at the electrodes when solutions conducted. Therefore we need an apparatus in which we can collect any gases formed at the electrodes when solutions are electrolysed (see Fig 12.4). Some typical results from this experiment are shown in Table 12.2.

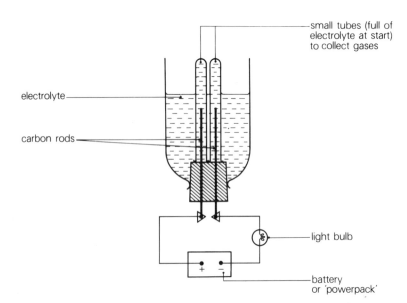

small tubes (full of electrolyte at start) to collect gases

electrolyte

carbon rods

light bulb

battery or 'powerpack'

Fig 12.4 The electrolysis of solutions

Substance	Cathode product	Anode product
copper chloride solution	copper (brown 'plating')	chlorine (green gas, smell)
lead nitrate solution	lead (metallic crystals)	oxygen (often hard to identify)*
potassium iodide solution	hydrogen ('pop' test)	iodine (gives a brown solution)
magnesium bromide solution	hydrogen ('pop' test)	bromine (gives a brown solution)
sodium sulphate solution	hydrogen ('pop' test)	oxygen (often hard to identify)*
dilute sulphuric acid (hydrogen sulphate solution)	hydrogen ('pop' test)	oxygen (often hard to identify)*

* if the electrode is made of carbon, the oxygen can react to produce carbon dioxide.

Table 12.2 Electrolysis of some solutions

There are some surprises here! Instead of metals at the cathode we sometimes get hydrogen. Except in the case of the dilute acid (which itself contains hydrogen), this must be coming from the water (hydrogen oxide). It can also be seen that metals high in the affinity series (see Chapter 9) are not deposited, whereas metals lower down are deposited.

At the anode we get the non-metal if this is chlorine, bromine or iodine; but we do not get sulphur or its compounds from sulphate, nor do we get nitrogen or its compounds from nitrate. Instead we get oxygen from the water. Here is a summary of the results of the electrolysis of solutions:

product at cathode – *either* the metal from the salt, *or* hydrogen (from the water) if the metal is high in the affinity series;

product at anode – chlorine, bromine or iodine if they are present, otherwise oxygen from the water.

12.4 Electroplating

The fact that some metals (those which are low in the

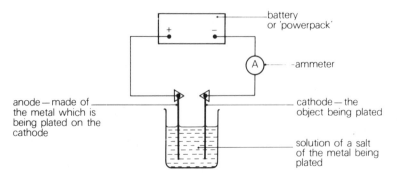

Fig 12.5 Electroplating

anode—made of the metal which is being plated on the cathode

battery or 'powerpack'

ammeter

cathode—the object being plated

solution of a salt of the metal being plated

affinity series) are deposited on the cathode is useful in **electroplating**, a very important technique in industry.

You can do simple electroplating yourself using a circuit as shown in Fig 12.5. It is found that a metal anode goes into solution when the current flows and thus the metal salt does not get more dilute during the experiment. To ensure that the plating is even, the current must be kept low or, more exactly, the ratio $\dfrac{\text{current}}{\text{area of object}}$ must be kept low. The object to be plated must be clean and free from grease. Ideally, special salts should be used. Copper and brass objects can be plated with nickel or zinc using this method.

Electroplating is widely used in the manufacture of metal objects as it enables a thin layer of an expensive metal to be plated on to a cheaper 'base metal'. For example, 'silver' cutlery which is marked 'EPNS' (electroplated nickel silver) has a layer of silver plated on to an alloy of copper, nickel and zinc. Many steel objects, such as car bumpers, are electroplated with chromium to improve their appearance and to stop corrosion.

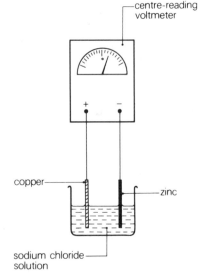

centre-reading voltmeter

copper

zinc

sodium chloride solution

Fig 12.6 An experiment to establish the electrochemical series

Further reading

For further reading on electrolysis see *Physics 11–13*, pages 218–222.

12.5 Electricity from chemical reactions

If a piece of copper and a piece of zinc are dipped in sodium

magnesium	—1.2 volts
zinc	—0.7 volts
iron	—0.3 volts
tin	—0.2 volts
copper	0
silver	+0.2 volts

Table 12.3 Some typical results when metals are paired with copper

chloride solution and connected up to a centre-reading voltmeter (Fig 12.6) a voltage is produced. If the zinc is replaced by magnesium, a larger voltage is produced on the same side of the zero. If the magnesium is now replaced by silver, the voltage changes to the other side of the zero. Two pieces of copper, of course, produce no voltage. Table 12.3 shows some typical results when various metals are paired with copper in this experiment.

If another metal is substituted for the copper, the voltage will be the difference between the readings in the table. For example, magnesium and zinc should produce about 0.5 volts and magnesium and silver should produce about 1.4 volts.

The order of the metals in Table 12.3 is called the **electrochemical series**; you will notice that the metals shown are in the same order as the affinity and displacement series (Chapter 9). The electrical measurements can be made very accurately and the electrochemical series can be used to separate metals which are very close in the displacement series. For example, nickel is found to be above tin.

The electrical energy comes from chemical reactions. This can be seen in the Daniell cell* (Fig 12.7a) which gives a voltage of 1.1 v. After the cell has been in use for a while the appearance of the zinc rod makes it clear that some zinc has been used up. If the copper can were dried and reweighed it would be found to have gained mass. The reaction which supplies the electrical energy here is:

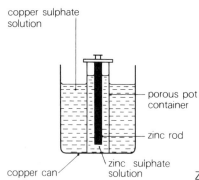

copper sulphate solution

porous pot container

zinc rod

copper can

zinc sulphate solution

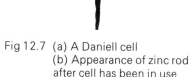

ZINC + COPPER SULPHATE → COPPER + ZINC SULPHATE

All batteries used in everyday life convert chemical energy into electrical energy. However, the chemical reactions which occur are often complicated. One of the commonest cells is the 'dry cell' (Fig 12.8). Here the chemical reaction is between zinc and manganese dioxide. The electrolyte is in the form of a paste, hence the cell is described as 'dry'.

Fig 12.7 (a) A Daniell cell
(b) Appearance of zinc rod after cell has been in use for a while

* A *cell* has just one pair of electrodes (for example zinc and copper in a Daniell cell). A *battery* consists of a number of cells joined together (see *Physics 11–13*, page 179).

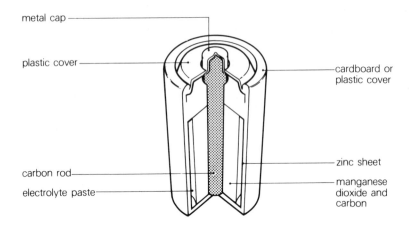

metal cap

plastic cover

cardboard or plastic cover

zinc sheet

carbon rod

electrolyte paste

manganese dioxide and carbon

Fig 12.8 A dry cell

Car batteries depend on the reaction of lead with brown lead oxide in the presence of sulphuric acid. The reaction may be reversed by forcing electricity back through the battery which means that the battery can be recharged, a most important point. Rechargeable batteries are known as **accumulators**.

Questions

1. Of the following which are good and which are very poor conductors?

a. Copper.
b. Iron.
c. Plastic.
d. Glass.
e. Carbon (graphite).
f. Water.
g. Ethanol.
h. Mercury.
i. Sugar solution.
j. Dilute sulphuric acid.
k. Solid sodium chloride.

l. Molten sodium chloride.
m. Sodium chloride solution.
n. Copper sulphate crystals.
o. Copper sulphate solution.

2.

a. What is the difference between a conductor and an electrolyte?

b. In Question 1, which of the conductors also behave as electrolytes?

3.

a. Draw a diagram to show how you would electrolyse a molten salt. Label the electrodes and the electrolyte.
b. What products would you expect at the cathode and the anode if you electrolysed:
   i Molten sodium bromide?
   ii Molten calcium chloride?
   iii Molten lead iodide?

4. When sodium chloride solution is electrolysed, hydrogen is obtained at the cathode and chlorine at the anode.
a. Where does the hydrogen come from?
b. How would you test for the hydrogen?
c. Suggest why sodium is *not* formed at the cathode.
d. What else might have been obtained at the anode?
e. Sketch a diagram of the apparatus you would use to collect the chlorine and hydrogen gases during electrolysis.

5.

a. Why does the electrolysis of copper sulphate solution produce copper at the cathode while potassium sulphate solution gives hydrogen at the cathode?
b. What would you expect to get at the cathode if silver nitrate solution were electrolysed?
c. What would you expect at the cathode if magnesium sulphate solution were electrolysed?

6. Write down the products you would expect at the cathode and anode when the following are electrolysed:
a. Molten potassium chloride.
b. Potassium chloride solution.
c. Sodium sulphate solution.
d. Dilute hydrochloric acid.
e. Copper nitrate solution.

7. When malachite reacts with sulphuric acid, a blue solution is produced (Section 11.6). One way of showing that this is a copper salt is to obtain copper from it by electrolysis.

137

a. Draw a diagram of the apparatus you would use for this experiment.
b. Where would you find copper?
c. What other substance would be produced during the electrolysis?
d. When limestone reacts with hydrochloric acid, a colourless solution is produced. What products are formed at the anode and cathode when this solution is electrolysed?

Background reading

Obtaining elements by electrolysis

There is no chemical way of making the very reactive elements, they have to be obtained from their compounds using electrolysis.

Of the non-metals, the most reactive is fluorine which comes off at the anode when a mixture of hydrogen fluoride and molten potassium fluoride is electrolysed. Fluorine is such a reactive gas that many common substances catch fire when they come into contact with it. It is not surprising that very little fluorine is made.

On the other hand almost a million tons of chlorine, the second most reactive non-metal, are manufactured in the United Kingdom each year. In this case the electrolyte is a solution of sodium chloride (brine). Chlorine is formed at the anode, hydrogen at the cathode and sodium hydroxide solution (caustic soda) is left behind.

SODIUM + HYDROGEN HYDROXIDE ⟶ CHLORINE + HYDROGEN + SODIUM
CHLORIDE   (water)   HYDROXIDE

The brine is often obtained from the salt left by ancient seas from which the water has evaporated. ICI make a large amount of chlorine in Cheshire.

Chlorine is used to make many of its compounds which have a wide variety of uses, such as plastics, drugs, anaesthetics, insecticides and solvents. Chlorine is also used to make another non-metal, bromine. The sea contains bromides which react with chlorine in a displacement reaction:

SODIUM BROMIDE + CHLORINE ⟶ BROMINE + SODIUM CHLORIDE

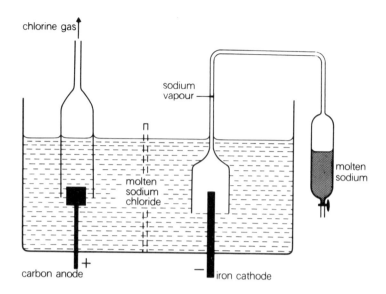

chlorine gas

sodium
vapour

molten
sodium

molten
sodium
chloride

Fig 12.9 The Downs process

carbon anode +

− iron cathode

There is a big bromine factory on the coast at Amlwch in Anglesey.

Although an *aqueous* solution of a chloride can be electrolysed to make chlorine, the reactive metals are made by electrolysing molten salts. If water were present, hydrogen (and not the metal) would be formed at the cathode. Sodium is produced using the Downs process. Sodium chloride is melted and electrolysed. Chlorine is produced at the anode and is kept apart from the molten sodium which comes off the cathode (see Fig 12.9).

Magnesium and aluminium are produced by similar methods. In the case of aluminium the electrolyte is a molten mixture of aluminium fluoride and aluminium oxide.

Electrolysis can also be used to produce very pure samples of less reactive metals such as copper (see Section 13.3).

Questions
1. Name two other metals (not sodium, magnesium or aluminium) which have to be made by electrolysis.
2. In the Downs process, why do you think the sodium and the chlorine have to be kept apart?

Chapter 13 **Metals from minerals**

Minerals are chemical substances found in rocks; they may be elements or, more often, compounds. Minerals from which metals can be obtained are called **ores**. We have already met two ores from which useful products can be obtained; malachite which gives us copper (Section 11.6) and limestone which leads to a wide range of 'lime' products (Section 11.7). To obtain metals from minerals, three stages are needed. First the ore has to be concentrated, for many ores are found embedded in useless rock. Then the metal has to be extracted chemically from the ore. Finally, the metal may have to be purified or made into an alloy.

13.1 Rocks and ores

Not all the elements are equally common on earth. Excluding the core (inside) of the earth, the approximate percentages (of the total mass) of the different elements are shown in Fig 13.1.

None of the other common everyday metals (copper, lead, tin, zinc) come in the top twenty and none are as common as 0.01%. You will notice that silicon and oxygen are by far the most common; rocks contain a great deal of silicon oxide (sand and quartz) as well as compounds known as silicates (which contain both silicon and oxygen) and alumino-silicates (containing aluminium, silicon and oxygen). These compounds have to be separated and removed from the more valuable mineral. This separation usually uses physical differences. For example, the ore can be crushed and the mineral separated from the useless rock using the fact that the rock and the mineral have very different densities.

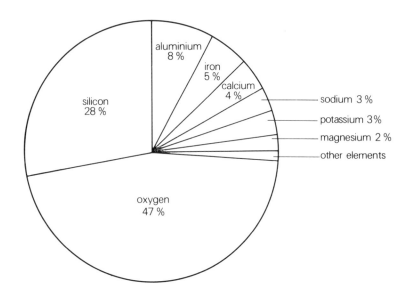

Fig 13.1 The composition of the earth's crust

13.2 Extraction of the metal

When the mineral has been concentrated, the problem now is to extract the metal. The method used depends on the position of the metal in the affinity series (Chapter 9 and Appendix 3). Metals that are very low in the series sometimes occur **native**: that is, as the pure metal. One such example is gold. Another unreactive metal is mercury which sometimes occurs native, but more often as compounds which decompose easily when they are heated, giving the metal.

The more reactive everyday metals (those between zinc and copper in the affinity series) have to be prepared by chemical reduction. The ore is often an oxide or else can easily be converted into an oxide. It is then a question of finding a reducing agent that can remove the oxygen from the oxide. The one that is used most often is carbon (coke, made by heating coal). It has the great advantage of being cheap, for coal can easily be dug out of the ground. In addition the oxide of carbon is a gas, which means that there is no problem about separating the metal and the carbon oxide, the products of the reaction. Coke is also strong and mixes well with the oxide that is to be reduced. In contrast, compare carbon with another possible reducing agent, aluminium. This is very expensive, for it has to be made using electrolysis; also, its oxide is a solid, which will make separation of the products difficult.

The very reactive metals (such as aluminium, magnesium and sodium) have to be prepared using electrolysis (Chapter 12). The molten salt is used as the electrolyte, as a solution would give only hydrogen at the cathode (Section 12.3).

13.3 Purification and alloy making

Having extracted our metal, we are faced with the problem of purification. The degree of purification will depend on what the metal is to be used for. It may involve further reduction, or electrolysis. For example, impure copper is made the anode of an electrolysis cell, with copper sulphate solution as the electrolyte (Fig 13.2). Copper leaves the anode and is *plated* on the cathode. The impurities either remain on the anode or dissolve into the solution, but they do not plate on to the cathode. The copper at the cathode is 99.9% pure.

Alloys are mixtures or compounds of metals with other elements. Steels, which are alloys of iron, are harder than iron because they contain the right amount of carbon. Steels that are used for special jobs often have other metals added as well; for example, stainless steel also contains chromium and nickel. Other alloys include brass (copper and zinc), bronze (copper and tin) and amalgams (mercury with other metals).

13.4 Iron

Iron is the most widely used metal, both by itself and in steels. It is quite common (Fig 13.1) and is made from its

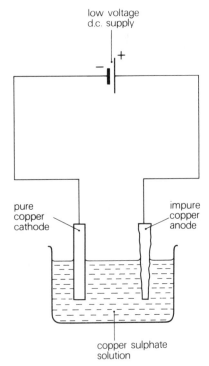

low voltage
d.c. supply

pure
copper
cathode

impure
copper
anode

copper sulphate
solution

Fig 13.2 Purifying copper by electrolysis

ores by reduction with carbon. The reaction is carried out in towers 60 metres high known as **blast furnaces**; these are also used in the making of lead and zinc (Fig 13.3). At the top of the furnace iron ore (iron oxide and rock), coke and limestone are fed in. At the bottom of the furnace hot air at 800°C is blasted in (hence the name) and this reacts with some of the coke to raise the temperature higher still. At the bottom of the furnace the temperature is about 1600°C, at which temperature the iron is liquid. The overall reaction is:

IRON OXIDE + CARBON ⟶ CARBON DIOXIDE + IRON

The rock in the ore would still be solid at this temperature and it would rapidly block up the furnace. The limestone is added to convert the rock to a liquid mixture called slag. One

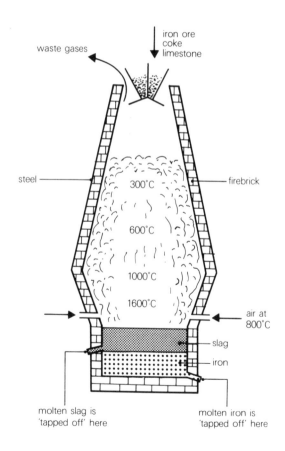

Fig 13.3 The blast furnace

Type	Percentage carbon	Description	Some uses
mild steel	0.1 – 0.2	fairly soft and malleable	boiler plates, rivets, nuts and bolts
medium carbon steel	0.2 – 0.7	less malleable and harder	rails, axles, castings
high carbon steel	0.7 – 1.5	not very malleable, but very hard	hammers, machine tools, cutting tools

Table 13.1 Uses of three types of steel

of the main substances in slag is calcium silicate which is formed from the silicon oxide in the rock:

$$\text{CALCIUM CARBONATE} \xrightarrow{\text{heat}} \text{CALCIUM OXIDE} + \text{CARBON DIOXIDE}$$
(limestone)

$$\text{CALCIUM OXIDE} + \text{SILICON OXIDE} \longrightarrow \text{CALCIUM SILICATE}$$
(solid) (solid) (liquid)

The slag floats on the iron (being less dense) and the liquid slag and the impure liquid iron (known as pig iron) are both run out of the furnace at intervals and then solidify. The slag can be used in road-making, though, too often in the past, it was piled up into heaps which spoilt the appearance of the landscape.

The impure pig iron contains 3–4% carbon from the coke and is very brittle. Much of this iron is turned into steel and this involves removing most of the carbon but leaving enough to give steel its strength. Steel is made by a number of processes, all of which involve oxidizing the excess carbon by blowing oxygen or air over or through molten iron. Different types of steel have different percentages of carbon (see Table 13.1).

13.5 Corrosion and its prevention

(See also Section 5.8.)

Although we can get metals from ores, the reverse process is the one that occurs naturally and we are always having to fight to prevent metals corroding. The higher a metal comes in the affinity series, the greater the corrosion problem can be. Indoors copper does not corrode and out-of-doors it is many years before a copper roof reacts with the gases in the atmosphere to give the beautiful green colour of the compounds that form on the surface of the copper. Iron, however, rusts much more rapidly and the following ways have been devised to prevent the rusting:

1. Make it into stainless steel (Section 13.3). This is expensive.
2. Paint it. This prevents the iron from coming into contact with the oxygen and water in the atmosphere.
3. Coat it (plate it) with a layer of a less reactive metal (such as tin or chromium) to keep away the oxygen and water.
4. Cover it with a more reactive metal (for example, galvanize it with zinc) so that the more reactive metal corrodes rather than the iron.

Corrosion is a considerable problem costing thousands of millions of pounds a year. It is worth spending money to prevent it, especially as a lot of money has been spent obtaining the metal from the ore in the first place.

Summary

1. The stages in obtaining a metal from a mineral are:
a. Concentration of the ore.
b. Chemical extraction of the metal.
c. Purification or alloy-making.
2. Metals low in the affinity series occur native. Everyday metals in the middle of the affinity series are extracted by carbon reduction of their oxides. Metals high in the affinity series are extracted by electrolysis of their molten salts.
3. Zinc, iron and lead are extracted from their ores by carbon reduction in a blast furnace.

Questions

1.
a. Which are the two most common elements in the earth's crust?
b. Which is the commonest metal?
c. What three stages have to be carried out to obtain a pure metal from an impure ore?

2.[†] Name a metal which:
a. Occurs naturally as a pure element.
b. Is normally obtained using electrolysis.
c. Is normally obtained by heating its oxide with carbon.

3.
a. Tin is found in tinstone (cassiterite, tin oxide) in Cornwall. Refer to Chapter 9 and then suggest how tin is made from tinstone.
b. Sodium is found as rock salt (sodium chloride) in Cheshire. Suggest how sodium is obtained from rock salt.

4.
a. Give as many reasons as you can why in industry carbon is a more useful reducing agent than magnesium.
b. Could hydrogen be used as an industrial reducing agent? Consider its advantages and disadvantages compared with carbon and magnesium.

5.
a. In a blast furnace what is the reason for:
    i The blast of hot air?
    ii The coke?
    iii The limestone?
b. What liquid products come out of the furnace?
c. Air is blasted in. What gases come out of the top of the furnace?

6. Suggest reasons why:
a. Lead, rather than iron, is used on church roofs.
b. Iron rusts very slowly in a desert, more quickly next to a freshwater lake, and very rapidly near the sea.
c. Copper, not the cheaper iron, is used for water pipes.
d. Iron greenhouse frames are painted with aluminium paint.
e. A steel car bumper rusts quickly if the chromium plating breaks.

7.[†] Give one advantage and one disadvantage in each case for the following uses for metals:
a. Silver for coins.
b. Lead for water pipes.
c. Iron for bridges.

8. In the thermit process, aluminium powder is mixed with the oxide of either iron or chromium or certain other metals. On ignition by a fuse the oxide is reduced to the metal, which is molten at the temperature of the reaction. Welding of steel rails can be carried out by packing a mixture of aluminium powder and iron oxide round the joint and igniting the mixture with a fuse.

a. What does this tell you about the relative positions of aluminium, iron and chromium in the affinity series?

b. Name another metal which could be extracted from its oxide using the thermit process.

c. Write a word-equation for the reaction between aluminium and chromium oxide.

d. Iron is not made commercially by the thermit process. Suggest a reason for this.

e. Explain what happens when the thermit process is used to weld steel rails together.

9.[†]

a. An ore of lead can be converted into lead oxide by heating, but heat alone will not convert it into the metal. If you were given some of the lead oxide, how would you try to obtain some metallic lead from it? Describe the experiment and say how you would know whether it had been successful.

b. When lead is melted in a crucible the shiny surface of the molten metal soon becomes tarnished. Suggest a reason for this, and suggest a way of melting lead without letting the surface become tarnished.

c. It is not difficult to obtain metallic lead from its ore, so why is lead sufficiently valuable for it to be worthwhile for thieves to steal it?

Background reading

Air pollution from metal manufacture

Anyone who has lived near an iron and steel works, or near a blast furnace which makes zinc or lead, will be aware of the problem of pollution. In these cases, the blast furnace gives off a lot of harmless carbon dioxide, but the ores often contain impurities which oxidize to harmful gases. The worst menace are ores containing sulphur, which will come out of the furnace as sharp-smelling sulphur dioxide. In the air this is converted into the very acidic sulphuric acid. This damages buildings and is harmful to plants and the lungs of those who breathe it. Power stations also give out sulphur dioxide from sulphur impurities in the coal or oil which they burn.

Together with these gases smoke will be formed; smoke consists of a lot of very small solid particles and these will be scattered in the area surrounding the factory. They may only be dirty and a nuisance, but, in the case of zinc and lead, they will be poisonous as well, as compounds of these metals are toxic to humans.

There is a tendency to blame 'the scientists' for this pollution. However, the real cause is man's increasing need for metals. Those who change their motor cars frequently or turn up their central heating thermostats are making blast furnaces and power stations work harder.

Scientists *can* control pollution. Recently the laws have been tightened up so that blast furnaces are not the menace they once were. However, such control is expensive and to eliminate pollution completely would be very expensive indeed. Pollution is part of the price we have to pay for the luxury of using so much energy and so many things which are made out of metal. But, like all prices, it should be kept as low as possible.

Revision questions

One-word answers

1. Choose words from the following to fill in the gaps below:

Boils, burns, combines, compound, condenses, decomposes, dissolves, filtrate, melts, mixes, solution, suspension.

a. When sulphur is heated it first .... to a yellow–brown liquid and then .... to form sulphur dioxide.

b. When copper carbonate is heated it .... into copper oxide and carbon dioxide.

c. When hydrogen burns in air it .... with oxygen to form water.

d. When sugar is shaken with water it .... to form a colourless ....

2. Fill each of the gaps in the following sentences with a suitable word.

a. If you stir your tea, the sugar will .... more quickly.

b. Puddles in the road disappear because the heat of the sun .... the water.

c. Substances that burn do so more fiercely in .... than in air.

3. In the short paragraph below six words have been omitted. Select the appropriate six words from the list of ten and insert them in the blanks.

Residue, filtrate, suspension, dissolves, mixture, decomposes, solution, precipitate, solute, compound.

If a small amount of a .... of salt and sand is shaken with some water in a beaker, the salt ...., forming a colourless .... If the contents of the beaker are filtered, the sand remains in the filter paper. The clear liquid which passes through the filter paper is known as the .... When the liquid is heated in an evaporating basin the solvent evaporates and eventually the ...., a .... of sodium and chlorine, is left in the basin as a dry white powder.

4. Copper, hydrated cobalt chloride crystals, hydrated copper sulphate crystals, magnesium, salt solution, sand, sulphur, water.

   From the list of substances above, choose the one which best fits each of the following descriptions:
   a. A metal which is partly converted to a black oxide when heated in air.
   b. A compound which changes from pink to blue when heated.
   c. A colourless liquid which boils at 100°C.
   d. A colourless liquid which, on heating, boils away and leaves a white residue behind.
   e. A non-metallic element which, on heating in air, burns to give a gas.
   f. A substance which neither burns, melts, nor boils when heated using a Bunsen burner.

5. Liquids A–D were investigated with universal indicator solution and the following results were obtained:

Liquid	Colour of the indicator
A	yellow
B	red
C	purple
D	green (pH 7)

   a. Which liquid could have been pure water?
   b. Which liquid could have been sodium hydroxide solution?
   c. B was produced by burning an element in air and dissolving the oxide in water. Suggest any element which could have formed B.
   d. What would be the approximate pH of A?
   e. Which of the four liquids would you use to change the pH of A to 7?

6. Carbon, copper, sodium, sulphur, zinc.
   From this list select:
a. An element which will *not* conduct electricity.
b. An element used on a large scale for extracting metals from their ores.
c. An element that would be suitable for adding to dilute acid to make hydrogen gas.
d. An element whose oxide makes an alkaline solution when added to water.

7. Fill in the gaps in the following sentences:
a. Copper oxide is a .... of copper and oxygen. If a mixture of copper oxide and carbon is heated, the gas called .... is formed, and the copper oxide is reduced to ....
b. The commonest (most abundant) gas in the atmosphere is ...., and the second most common gas is .... One difference between air and pure oxygen is that the latter will make a glowing splint ....

8. Name one example of each of the following found outside the laboratory.
a. An acidic substance.
b. An alkaline substance.
c. Large quantities of condensed water vapour.
d. Carbon.

Longer answers

9. Suggest what is happening in the following experiments:
a. If a little lead oxide is mixed with powdered charcoal and heated strongly on asbestos paper, some tiny shining beads soon appear in the mixture.
b. A solution X turns indicator paper blue (pH 11), but when solution Y is added to the solution X the mixture turns indicator paper red (pH 2).
c. If an alum crystal is hung in a solution of alum in water it may sometimes get smaller and disappear instead of growing larger.
d. If some petrol is carefully distilled, the temperature at which it boils gradually rises.

10. The table shows some of the physical properties of a number of substances.

	Melting point (°C)	Boiling point (°C)	Solubility in water
sodium bromide	747	1390	soluble
aluminium oxide	2045	3000	insoluble
toluene	−95	111	insoluble
methane	−182	−160	insoluble
benzene	5	80	insoluble

a. Which of these substances is a gas at room temperature?
b. How would you recover aluminium oxide from a mixture of aluminium oxide and sodium bromide?
c. How would you separate benzene from water?
d. How would you attempt to separate benzene from a mixture of benzene and toluene?
e. Suggest a method of purifying aluminium oxide that has been contaminated with benzene.

11.
a. What is the name of the process used in the refining of crude oil?
b. Three products that can be obtained from crude oil are butane, eicosane and octane.

	butane	eicosane	octane
Melting point (°C)	−138	+37	−57
Boiling point (°C)	−1	+344	+125

In what form (solid, liquid or gas) would each product be at room temperature?
c. Which one of the three products:
  i Would not burn easily?
  ii Is most suitable as a fuel for motor cars?
  iii Could be used as a grease?

d. Some crude oils contain a substance which melts at 113°C and boils at 445°C. It burns to form one product only, an acidic gas. The substance itself does not conduct electricity.
  i Why do you think the substance is an element?
  ii Give two reasons why you think the element is a non-metal.

12.† The following passage is taken from an article on 'Safety in the Home'.
  'Fat for cooking is normally used at about 200°C at which temperature it is quite safe. If fat is heated above 240°C, however, a blue smoke is produced above the fat and this easily ignites. Burning fat accounts for about 40% of fire accidents in the home. If fat catches fire it should be covered with a pan lid or a damp cloth (after the gas or electricity has been switched off). It is important that water should not be thrown on to burning fat.'
  a. When food is boiled in water, at about what temperature is it cooked?
  b. Why is it usually quicker to cook food by frying rather than by boiling?
  c. Why is it important not to heat fat above 240°C?
  d. What would happen to a drop of water put into fat at 200°C?
  e. What therefore would be the result of throwing water on to burning fat?
  f. Explain why covering a pan of burning fat with a damp cloth or a lid will put out the fire.

13. The diagram (Fig 14.1) shows an experiment to investigate the burning of gas in air.
  a. Why does the container A have to be cold?
  b. What is the liquid collected in the basin B?
  c. How would you test the liquid to show that your answer to part b. was correct?

14. When two drops of a blue liquid are mixed with a little colourless vinegar in a test tube, the solution becomes yellow. A solution of two drops of the same liquid in limewater is blue.

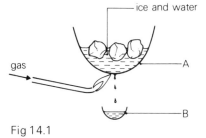

ice and water

gas

A

B

Fig 14.1

a. What colour would result if the blue liquid were added to a colourless solution known to go purple (pH 14) with universal indicator?
b. When you blow gently through a tube into a solution of the liquid in water, the blue colour is gradually replaced by yellow. What does this suggest about the air you breathe out? Suggest what gas in your breath might have caused the colour change.

15. Some shiny strips of copper were put into each of five corked test tubes and heated. Describe, giving your reasons, what you think would happen in each case.
a. The first test-tube contained air.
b. The second test-tube contained an inactive gas like nitrogen.
c. The third test-tube contained steam.
d. The fourth test-tube had all the air removed after the copper was put in. After heating, the test-tube was allowed to cool before being opened.
e. The fifth test-tube had all the air removed after the copper was put in, but the test-tube was opened before the test-tube had cooled down.

16. When a certain element R is strongly heated in air it burns forming a white powder.
a. If none of it is lost, do you think that the powder will weigh more or less than R?
b. Give a reason for your answer.
c. If some of the white powder is placed on wet indicator paper the colour of the paper changes to dark blue, indicating a pH of about 11.
     What word is used to describe a solution of pH 11?
d. Name one particular substance which might be added to a solution of pH 11 in order to lower its pH.
e. What word is used to describe a solution of pH 7?
f. Do you think that the element R is a metal or a non-metal? Explain your answer.
g. What do you think might happen to R if it were heated in a vacuum instead of in air?

17. An unknown element Q was heated in oxygen. The gaseous oxide which was formed was passed into water. The resulting solution was found to be acidic when tested with universal indicator paper.

a. What do you understand by the word element?
b. Was Q a metal or a non-metal?
   Give a reason for your answer.
c. When magnesium ribbon was added to some of the acidic solution in a test tube, a colourless gas was evolved. Draw a diagram of a suitable experimental arrangement for producing and collecting the colourless gas.
d. What gas would you expect to have been formed when the magnesium was added?
e. How would you test for this gas? What would happen if the test were successful?

18. A boy found that a white substance that had been given to him could not be separated into different substances by filtration, crystallization, chromatography or by heat. He then concluded that it must be an element.

a. Explain clearly why this conclusion was not justified.
b. Suggest two possible substances which the white substance might have been.
c. How would you distinguish between the two?

19. Here are four sets of substances.
   1 – Sodium chloride, lead oxide, copper sulphate.
   2 – Air, sea water, crude oil.
   3 – Carbon, sulphur, oxygen, nitrogen.
   4 – Sodium, magnesium, iron, lead.
Which set consists of:

a. Metallic elements?
b. Non-metallic elements?
c. Compounds?
d. Mixtures?
e. Choose one of the compounds and state how you would attempt to obtain a metallic element from it.

20.
a. Say whether you think each of the following is an element, a compound, or a mixture:
   Copper sulphate, air, water, beer, iron filings, vinegar, carbon, lead oxide.

b. For one of the compounds, describe briefly how you would try to obtain a sample of one of the elements in it.
c. For one of the mixtures, describe briefly how you would try to obtain a sample of one of the substances in it.

21.
a. What is the black material A deposited on the outside of a beaker which is placed over a wavering, yellow Bunsen burner flame?
    Is the air hole of the burner open or closed when this type of flame is produced?
b. What is the black material B deposited on the outside of a folded strip of copper after it has been held over a roaring Bunsen flame for several minutes?
    Why will the inside of the strip not have turned black?
c. What would happen if the following were heated using a roaring Bunsen flame?
    i Solid A.
    ii Solid B.
    iii A mixture of Solid A and Solid B.

22. Suggest reasons for the following observations:
a. When a kettle full of cold water is put on a gas burner to boil, the outside of the kettle soon becomes clouded with moisture which disappears again after a few minutes.
b. When the red juice from some stewed blackcurrants is spilt onto a starched linen tablecloth, the stain becomes blue in colour.
c. When a blob of ink is removed from a desk using the corner of a piece of blotting paper, the edge of the stain produced on the blotting paper often appears different in colour from the middle of it.
d. Objects made of brass usually need regular cleaning, but a brass clock under a glass dome needs to be cleaned only every few years.

23. Suggest why:
a. Many common indigestion remedies contain sodium bicarbonate, a mild alkali.
b. 35% of the air dissolved in water is oxygen, while the air itself contains only 20% of oxygen.

c. Glass is widely used for making scientific apparatus.

24. Write four sentences, each using a different one of the words listed below. The sentences should convey some idea of the meaning of the words involved.
Ore, solvent, decompose, anhydrous.

25. Explain, giving examples, the differences between the following pairs of words:
a. Melting and dissolving.
b. Heating and burning.
c. Element and compound.

Appendix 1

An alphabetical list of the more common elements together with some of their properties

Name	Symbol	Discovered	Melts (°C)	Boils (°C)	Density (g/cm³)	Description
aluminium	Al	1827	660	2640	2.7	reactive metal
antimony	Sb	BC	630	1700	6.7	soft everyday metal
argon	Ar	1894	−189	−186	gas	non-metal (noble gas)
arsenic	As	1250	sublimes	613	5.7	properties in between those of metal and non-metal
barium	Ba	1808	710	1640	3.5	reactive metal
bromine	Br	1826	−7	58	3.1	red non-metal
calcium	Ca	1808	850	1480	1.6	reactive metal
carbon	C	BC	sublimes	4800	2.2	black non-metal
chlorine	Cl	1774	−101	−35	gas	pale green non-metal
chromium	Cr	1797	1900	2670	7.2	everyday metal
cobalt	Co	1735	1490	2900	8.9	everyday metal
copper	Cu	BC	1080	2570	8.9	brown everyday metal
fluorine	F	1886	−240	−188	gas	pale yellow non-metal
gold	Au	BC	1064	2800	19.3	yellow everyday metal
helium	He	1868	−270	−269	gas	non-metal (noble gas)
hydrogen	H	1766	−259	−253	gas	non-metal
iodine	I	1811	sublimes	183	4.9	dark purple non-metal
iron	Fe	BC	1540	2900	7.9	everyday metal
krypton	Kr	1898	−157	−153	gas	non-metal (noble gas)
lead	Pb	BC	327	1750	11.4	soft everyday metal
lithium	Li	1817	180	1330	0.5	reactive metal
magnesium	Mg	1808	650	1100	1.7	reactive metal
manganese	Mn	1774	1250	2000	7.4	everyday metal
mercury	Hg	BC	−39	357	13.6	everyday metal
neon	Ne	1898	−249	−246	gas	non-metal (noble gas)
nickel	Ni	1751	1450	2800	8.9	everyday metal
nitrogen	N	1772	−210	−196	gas	non-metal
oxygen	O	1774	−219	−183	gas	non-metal
phosphorus	P	1669	44	280	1.8	non-metal
platinum	Pt	1735	1770	4000	21.4	everyday metal
plutonium	Pu	1940	640	3200	19.8	radioactive metal
potassium	K	1807	64	760	0.9	reactive metal
radium	Ra	1898	700	1200	5.0	radioactive reactive metal
silicon	Si	1824	1410	2400	2.4	non-metal
silver	Ag	BC	961	2200	10.5	everyday metal
sodium	Na	1807	98	890	1.0	reactive metal
strontium	Sr	1808	770	1380	2.6	reactive metal
sulphur	S	BC	113	445	2.1	yellow non-metal
tin	Sn	BC	232	2600	7.3	soft everyday metal

Name	Symbol	Discovered	Melts (°C)	Boils (°C)	Density (g/cm³)	Description
titanium	Ti	1791	1670	3300	4.5	everyday metal
tungsten	W	1783	3400	6000	19.3	everyday metal
uranium	U	1841	1130	3800	19.0	radioactive metal
vanadium	V	1801	1900	3400	6.0	everyday metal
xenon	Xe	1898	−112	−108	gas	non-metal (noble gas)
zinc	Zn	1746	419	910	7.1	everyday metal

Notes on the Description column:
1. For the meanings of some of the words used, see Section 8.2.
2. Colours are only given for:
   gases which are not colourless,
   solids which are not grey.

Appendix 2

The preparation of common gases, with their tests

Gas	Preparation	Test	Observation
oxygen (Section 4.2)	1. Run hydrogen peroxide solution on to black manganese oxide (Fig 14.2). The manganese oxide *catalyses* (helps) the decomposition of the hydrogen peroxide to give oxygen. 2. Heat red lead oxide or potassium permanganate (Fig 4.1).	glowing splint	splint rekindles
carbon dioxide (Section 4.3)	1. Run dilute hydrochloric acid on to marble chips (Fig 14.3). 2. Heat a carbonate (Fig 4.3).	limewater	limewater turns milky
hydrogen (Chapter 10)	Run dilute sulphuric acid on to granulated zinc (Fig 14.4).	lighted splint	burns, often with typical 'pop'
steam (water) (Section 4.1)		melting point boiling point cobalt chloride paper anhydrous copper sulphate	0°C 100°C blue to pale pink white to blue

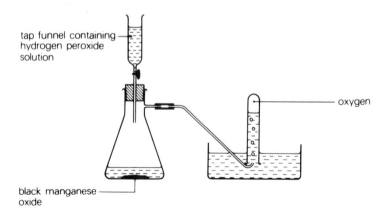

tap funnel containing hydrogen peroxide solution

oxygen

black manganese oxide

Fig 14.2 The preparation of oxygen

160

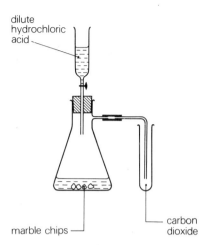

dilute
hydrochloric
acid

marble chips

carbon
dioxide

Fig 14.3 The preparation of carbon
dioxide

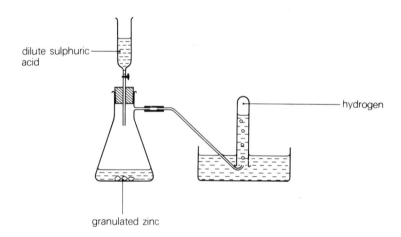

dilute sulphuric
acid

hydrogen

granulated zinc

Fig 14.4 The preparation of
hydrogen

Appendix 3

The positions of some common metals in the affinity series

Metal	Action of air	Action of water	Action of dilute acid	Action on oxide of carbon	hydrogen	Method of extraction from ore
potassium sodium calcium magnesium aluminium zinc iron tin lead copper mercury silver gold	burn readily to form oxides react slowly to form oxides no reaction	react with cold water to give metal hydroxide react with steam to give metal oxide and hydrogen no reaction	violent reactions **(danger)** react to form salt plus hydrogen no reaction	no reaction reduction occurs at high temperatures reduction occurs at 'Bunsen temperatures' heating, on its own, decomposes these oxides	no reaction some reduction reduction occurs	electrolysis of molten compound chemical reduction of ore (often using carbon) occur native

The position of carbon – at 'Bunsen temperatures' (up to about 800°C) it comes between tin and iron. As the temperature is raised, carbon is capable of reducing the oxides of metals higher in the series.

The position of hydrogen – hydrogen is on a very similar level to iron. Thus iron reacts with steam, but hydrogen has some reaction with iron oxide as well.

Appendix 4

The meaning of some important words often used in chemistry

Words in *italics* are themselves mentioned in the list.

A – adjective; N – noun; V – verb.

acid, N (or A): a sour substance with a *pH* less than 7, containing hydrogen which can be replaced by a metal.

affinity, N: the 'liking' of one element for another. Usually met in the 'affinity of metals for oxygen' leading to the **affinity series**.

alkali, N (A – **alkaline**): a *base* which is soluble in water. A substance which will *neutralize* an *acid* and which has a *pH* greater than 7.

alloy, N: a mixture of two or more metals.

analysis, N: finding out what a substance is.

anhydrous, A: without water. Used to describe *salts* which are not *hydrated*.

anode, N: the positive *electrode* in *electrolysis*.

base, N (A – **basic**): a substance which will *neutralize* an acid. Some bases are insoluble in water, others are soluble and called *alkalis*.

burning, N: the combination of a substance with oxygen, accompanied by a flame.

boiling point, N: the temperature at which a substance turns from liquid to gas.

cathode, N: the negative *electrode* in *electrolysis*.

chemical reaction, N: a process in which the *products* are different chemicals from the *reactants*.

chromatography, N: a method of separating coloured substances using a moving *solvent*.

combustion, N: the combination of a substance with oxygen.

compound, N: two or more elements chemically combined together.

condensation, N: a gas turning into a liquid.

decomposition, N: a *chemical reaction* in which a *compound* breaks down into simpler substances, usually as a result of being heated.

density, N: the mass of a particular volume of a substance. Usually measured in g/cm^3.

displacement, N: the 'pushing out' of a metal from one of its salts by another metal.

distillate, N: the result of *distillation*.

distillation, N: the *evaporation* and *condensation* of a liquid. Used to separate the *solvent* from a *solution*.

dissolving, N: the process by which a *solution* is formed.

electrochemical series, N: a list of metals, arranged in order of the voltages they produce when placed in pairs in an *electrolyte*.

electrode, N: a conducting rod by which the current enters or leaves an *electrolyte*.

electrolysis, N: the *decomposition* of a substance caused by an electric current.

electrolyte, N : the substance which is *decomposed* in *electrolysis*.

element, N : a substance which cannot be broken down into a simpler substance by chemical means.

evaporation, N : the process of turning a liquid into a gas.

filtrate, N : the clear liquid or solution resulting from *filtration*.

filtration, N : the process of removing the solid particles from a *suspension* using a 'sieve'.

flame test, N : recognizing certain metals in *salts* using the colour they give to a flame.

flammable, A : catches fire easily.

fractional distillation, N : the separation of a mixture of liquids by *distilling* off those with different *boiling points* at different times.

fraction, N : a mixture of liquids which have boiling points within a small range of temperature, produced as a result of *fractional distillation*.

freeze, V : turn from a liquid into a solid.

hydrated, A : describes a *salt* which has water as part of its chemical structure.

insoluble, A : describes a substance which will not *dissolve* in a certain *solvent*.

immiscible, A : describes two liquids which stay as two layers when shaken together.

indicator, N : anything which 'indicates' – often used of substances which are different colours in *acids* and *alkalis*.

malleable, A : describes a *metal*'s *property* of being flexible and able to bend without breaking.

melt, V : change from solid to liquid. The temperature at which this occurs is called the **melting point**.

metals, N : a name given to one set of *elements*. They can be recognized by their *properties* (particularly: shiny when cut, *malleable*, form oxides which are *bases*).

mineral, N : naturally occurring substance of which rocks are made.

mixture, N : substances which are just mixed together, not chemically combined.

native, A : describes the state of an element which is found in rocks as the element itself, rather than as a compound.

neutralization, N : a reaction in which an *acid* and a *base* react together to form a *salt* and water.

non-metal part : the part of a *salt* which is not a metal : for example, chloride or sulphate.

ore, N : a solid *mineral* from which a metal can be obtained.

oxidation, N : the reaction of a substance with oxygen.

permanent change, N : a change which cannot easily be reversed.

pH : a scale of numbers describing *acidity* and *alkalinity*. pH 7 is described as neutral. Acids have pH values below 7, alkalis have pH values greater than 7.

properties, N : a description of a substance and how it behaves : **physical properties** include *density, melting point* and *malleability*; **chemical properties** describe the *chemical reactions* of a substance.

164

precipitate, N : a solid substance which is produced rapidly when two clear solutions are mixed.

product, N : the result of a *chemical reaction*.

pure substance, N : a single element or compound. All of it will melt at the same temperature.

reactant, N : a substance which takes part in a *chemical reaction*.

reduction, N : the removal of oxygen from a substance.

residue, N : something which is left behind. Usually **either** what remains on the filter paper after *filtration* **or** what is left after a substance has been heated.

salt, N : a compound which can be formed as the result of a *neutralization* reaction.

saturated solution, N : a solution in which no more solute will dissolve.

solute, N : a substance which *dissolves* in a *solvent*. It is said to be **soluble**.

solution, N : a liquid which has a solid (or another liquid) mixed with it. The particles are too small to be seen.

solvent, N : a liquid in which certain other substances *dissolve*.

sublime, V : to turn straight from solid to gas.

suspension, N : a mixture of solid particles in a liquid which will settle out if left for a while.

vapour, N : a gas which can easily be *condensed* to a liquid.

volatile, A : describes a substance which has a low boiling point.

viscous, A : sticky, treacly.

Index